Adulting Like a Boss
Life Skills for Tweens, Teens, and Young Adults

Sarah Powell

BEACON & QUILL
PUBLISHING LLC.

Beacon & Quill Publishing LLC

Contents

Introduction

I distinctly remember the look of confusion and shock that came across my mom's face. Then suddenly she was trying to hold back a laugh. We had a young guy in his first year of college staying in a room in our basement. My mom had asked him several times now to please keep his bathroom in the basement clean, and she had furnished him with all of the supplies he needed to do just that. Today my mom brought it up to him again, "Hey, I noticed you still haven't had a chance to clean your bathroom. Do you think you could get that done today?"

He immediately defended himself, "Actually, I've poured that cleaner you gave me into the toilet several different times now, but it never does anything. It's not working."

This was the response that brought about my mom's rapid shift from confusion to shock to amusement. At the same moment, we all realized with a twinge of embarrassment that this poor guy had no idea how to clean a toilet. He'd never done it in his life. My mom held back her laughter and walked him down to the basement to demonstrate how to use a toilet brush. No, the toilet does not magically clean itself when you pour the cleaner in; you must also use the magical wand known as a toilet brush (or Johnny Mop, if you prefer), and put some elbow grease into it. We won't even talk about when we had to teach him to use the stove to boil water... Lucky for that guy, my mom was there to help him out, since he didn't have a handy-dandy guide like the one you're holding now.

That's why I wrote "Adulting Like a Boss: Life Skills for Tweens, Teens, and Young Adults." This book is here to be your trusty guide, helping you navigate the sometimes confusing, often hilarious, and always important journey to adulthood. It's crafted especially for those of you aged 13-23, but also for parents, teachers, and anyone else who wants to arm young people with the skills they need to succeed.

What can you expect to find here? A little bit of everything you need to know but might not have learned in school. We'll cover personal finance because—yes—money matters. Cooking and nutrition will teach you to make something more than instant noodles. Time management will help you balance your Netflix time with homework. Household maintenance will show you how to avoid the toilet brush introduction scenario. And there's more: health and wellness, job skills, communication skills, emotional intelligence, internet safety, and even automobile basics.

Why are these skills so important? Let's break it down. Most schools focus on academics but leave out practical life skills. This gap means that lots of young adults enter the world without knowing how to budget, cook, or even change a tire. Learning these skills early not only makes you more self-sufficient but can also lead to a happier, more successful life. It's like having a toolbox that's always ready for any challenge.

To make learning fun and engaging, I've included all kinds of tools in this book. You'll find easy diagrams, illustrations, and checklists. These aren't just to look pretty; they're designed to help you put what you learn into practice. Each chapter invites you to roll up your sleeves and try things out for yourself.

So, here's my call to action for you: dive in with an open mind. Try the exercises, apply the tips, and don't be afraid to make mistakes. Share your progress with friends and family. Make this book your secret weapon in the quest for adulthood.

Are you ready? Let's get started on this journey together. You've got this!

Chapter 1

Mastering Personal Finance

R emember the first time you got your hands on a bit of cash? Whether it was from mowing lawns or a birthday card stuffed with crisp bills, it felt like you'd just been granted a one-way ticket to a land of endless possibilities. You could buy that video game, maybe a bucket-load of gummy bears, or whatever else your heart desired. But then, before you knew it, poof! That money vanished faster than a Snapchat story. That moment, my friend, is exactly why mastering personal finance is crucial. This chapter is all about learning the ropes of managing money, so it doesn't pull a disappearing act on you.

Managing your finances is not just about stashing cash under your mattress. It's about creating a realistic budget—a plan that balances your income and expenses, keeping stress off your shoulders and your wallet happily plump. Think of a budget like your personal financial GPS. It shows you where your money is coming from and where it's going, so you can avoid the dreaded surprise of an empty bank account when you least expect it. A budget is your secret weapon against overspending, and a reliable friend that helps you save up for that shiny new phone or that unforgettable road trip with friends.

Creating a Realistic Budget

Let's get down to the nitty-gritty. A budget is simply a plan for your money. It's a way to track what you earn and what you spend. Picture it as a map that guides every dollar to its rightful place, ensuring you don't find yourself in a pickle when you need cash for something important. Tracking income and expenses is the cornerstone of effective money management. It's like counting calories for your wallet, helping you make healthier financial choices. By keeping tabs on your spending, you can prevent impulse buys that lead to buyer's remorse and start saving for your future.

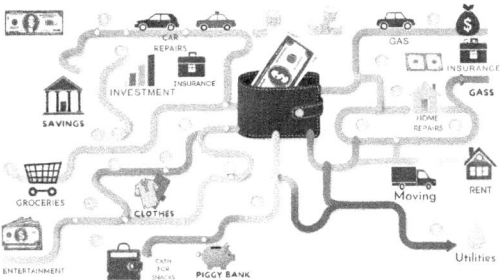

So, how do you create this magical thing called a budget? First, list all your sources of income. This could be your weekly allowance, earnings from a part-time job, or even that crisp twenty your grandma slipped into your hand on your last visit. Next, categorize your expenses. Divide them into two groups: needs and wants. Needs are the essentials like deodorant, school supplies, and phone bills. Wants are those tempting extras like movie tickets and late-night pizza runs. Setting realistic limits for each category is key. Don't starve your wants entirely, because let's be honest, everyone deserves a little fun. Use budgeting tools or apps to track everything the easy way (or a spreadsheet if you want to go really old school). Apps like Monarch, YNAB, or Toshl are fantastic for teens, providing user-friendly interfaces to keep your finances in check (Caldera, 2024). And if you don't have any income yet, don't worry. Go ahead and start tracking your expenses for needs and wants so that you can get an idea of how much income you want to work towards to afford what you'd like. That will help you figure out what kind of a job and how many hours of work you should start looking for.

As an example, you could start by listing your income sources, such as a weekly allowance of $20 and a part-time job bringing in $50 weekly. With that total of $70 per week coming in, you can now divide up where to spend the money on different expenses. You might set aside $25 for school supplies, $25 for entertainment, and aim to save $20 each week toward the new shoes you've been eyeing online. Break it down into monthly and weekly goals to make it feel less daunting. Scan the QR code to access a sample budge template to get you started. Save a copy of the template to your device before you start making edits. This template is just a starting point—feel free to tweak it to fit your unique financial landscape:

 Sticking to a budget might sound like a drag, but it's easier than you think with a few practical tips. Regularly review and update your budget. Life changes—so should your budget. If you notice any unnecessary expenses, cut them out like a bad haircut. Prioritize saving a portion of your income first, before spending, so you're always prepared for those rainy days. Remember, budgeting doesn't mean depriving yourself. It means making sure your money works for you, not against you. And if you plan fun money into the

budget, then instead of keeping you back from fun spending, your budget should help you make sure you always have money for the fun opportunities that come up.

Creating a budget is your first step towards financial independence. It's about making informed choices and avoiding those (often regrettable) impulse buys. So grab a notebook, or download an app, and start plotting out where your money should go. It's time to turn those dreams into goals and those goals into reality. It's not just about numbers; it's about building a life where you're in control.

Saving for Short and Long-Term Goals

Back to those new shoes we mentioned saving for a second ago, the ones that make your heart flutter every time you see them in the Instagram ads. You've been dreaming of holding them, wearing them, making them yours. But there's a twist to this story—the price tag. That's where saving comes in, both to fulfill short-lived desires and also to build a safety net for the unexpected and plan for those big life moments we all look forward to. Saving is like planting seeds for your future; with a little patience and care, those seeds can grow into something amazing.

First things first, let's talk about why saving is so important. Picture this: your bike's tire blows out, and you need a replacement ASAP. An emergency fund is your go-to stash for these unplanned expenses. It's a stress-buster, ready to swoop in when life throws you a curveball. Then there are your short-term goals, like saving for that new gear or maybe a trip with friends. Saving isn't just about holding on to money; it's about being ready for whatever comes next, like college tuition or even a down payment on a house. The earlier you start saving, the more secure your financial future will be (Karr, 2024).

Setting savings goals might sound intimidating, but it's all about being SMART. That means making goals that are Specific, Measurable, Achievable, Relevant, and Time-bound. (Check out Chapter 3 for a deeper dive into what SMART goals are.) Instead of  saying, "I want to save money," try, "I will save $100 in two months for a new game console." Visualizing your goals can help too. Create a vision board or use savings trackers to watch your progress unfold. Seeing your goals can make them feel real and within reach and help you stay motivated to keep saving.

As you start taking charge of your finances, you will also want to look into getting a bank account if you don't have one already. Opening your first bank account is a big step, so it's smart to shop around for the best option! If you are under 18, you'll need to open an account with a parent or legal guardian. Most banks offer some kind of special joint account options for minors that you can easily change into a private account when you turn 18, so get some information about what your parents' bank offers. If you're not going with your parents' bank, start by deciding between a bank and a credit union. Banks are bigger, have lots of locations, and often provide better options for travel spending, but their fees can be higher. Credit unions, on the other hand, are smaller, not-for-profit institutions that tend to offer lower fees and better interest rates because they're member-owned (National Credit Union Administration [NCUA], 2023). Look closely at services—do they offer a free checking account for young people? What about ATM access or mobile deposits? If you're into travel, does your bank let you spend money in foreign currencies without extra fees? Watch out for sneaky fees like overdraft charges or monthly account maintenance fees. Some accounts are free as long as you set up direct deposit or maintain a minimum balance. Finally, think about customer service. You want a place that's easy to reach and willing to answer your questions—this is your money, after all, so ask lots of questions and make sure you feel comfortable with where it's being kept!

Now, let's get practical with some saving strategies. One effective method is automatic transfers to a savings account. It's like setting your money on autopilot—no need to think about it; just let it grow. With most banks, you can set up a certain amount to be moved to your savings account on a specific day every month directly through your banking app. Pro tip—make that day the same as your payday so that there's no chance the money disappears before it makes it to the savings account. The "pay yourself first" method is another gem. Treat your savings like a bill that needs to be paid every month before anything else. This is essentially the same idea as automatic transfers, but you do the transfer yourself first thing on payday instead of it being automatic. You can also set up more than one savings account, usually at no extra charge. This is helpful if you want to save for more than one goal. For example, you might have one account for emergency funds, one account for a summer vacation trip fund, and one account to save for a new phone. This lets you keep different goals separate and makes it easy to see the progress being made toward each one individually. And if you deal a lot in cash, don't underestimate the power of loose change. Tossing coins into a jar might seem old school, but it can add up fast.

When it comes to where to stash your savings, you've got options. A regular savings account is a good starting point, offering easy access to your funds. This is often the best type of account to put emergency savings in because you can access it quickly if the need arises. If you're in it for the long haul, consider a high-yield savings account. It's like a regular savings account but often requires a higher initial deposit to open and provides a little extra boost in interest. For those who can wait a bit longer, certificates of deposit (CDs) might be worth a look. They often offer higher interest rates if you're willing to lock your money away and not be able to access it for a set period of time. (Interest rate refers to a percentage that the bank will pay into your savings each month as a kind of "thank you" for keeping your money in savings with them; higher interest rate = higher earnings over time.) Talking to your bank about the different savings options they offer is a great way to start if this is all new to you. They can break everything down for you and give you real numbers so you can see what your potential return would be for different types of savings plans.

As you look ahead to major milestones, having a savings plan is key. Whether it's college, a wedding, or buying your first home, start setting aside funds now. It might seem far off, but small steps today lead to big achievements tomorrow. And if retirement is on your horizon, even though it feels light-years away, it's never too early to start thinking about it. The earlier you invest in your future, the more comfortable it will be.

If you've already set up a savings plan with your bank, and you are still looking to do more, you can consider getting a Roth IRA, starting a 401K contribution, or talking to a financial advisor. Financial advisors are like personal trainers for your money, helping you navigate the financial maze, and they can help you go deeper into the world of investing. You'll find different types of advisors—fee-only, commission-based, and more—each with unique advantages. When choosing one, ask lots of questions about their fees, experience, and how they can help you reach your goals. The right advisor can be a valuable ally in your financial journey.

Now, armed with these insights, you're on your way to becoming a savvy saver. It's all about making informed choices, setting goals, and being prepared for anything life throws your way.

Understanding Credit and Debit Cards

Ah, plastic money—the thing that makes you feel like a financial wizard until the bill arrives. Credit and debit cards might look identical, but they operate in entirely different realms. Imagine a credit card as borrowing from your future self or, more accurately, from your future paychecks. When you swipe it, you're essentially taking a mini-loan from the bank, which you'll pay back later, hopefully before interest rates make it feel like you're buying that same thing twice. A debit card, on the other hand, is like having your wallet in card form. Swipe it, and the money comes straight out of your bank account, no strings attached—except for the sad reality of having less cash.

Using a credit card responsibly is like walking a tightrope. If you don't pay off your full balance each month, that balance starts building interest. That means the credit card company will charge you extra for every dollar you weren't able to pay back in full each month. A $5 purchase that isn't paid off can quickly become a $25 debt. Do it right, and you can build a solid credit history, which is like a golden ticket for future financial ventures. You will usually need a good credit score to get a vehicle loan, qualify for a house mortgage, or rent an apartment later. (Read more about credit scores in Chapter 14.) Pay off your balance in full each month to avoid paying interest. Think of it as clearing your tab before it morphs into a monstrous debt. Keep track of your spending, so you don't end up with a statement that gives you heart palpitations because you spent way more than you can pay off. And always read the fine print—interest rates and fees are the sneaky goblins of credit card land, ready to pounce if you're not vigilant. Use calendar reminders to pay your credit card bill so that you don't end up with unexpected interest because you forgot to pay on time. Or better yet, set up an automatic payment for the statement balance to come directly out of your bank account every month. This will guarantee you never end up paying interest; however, this only works if you make sure that you don't spend more on your credit card than you actually have in your bank account. If the credit card company goes to automatically withdraw the balance amount and there isn't enough in your account, then you'll have overdraft fees from your bank, which will be just as bad or worse than paying interest (*Credit Cards for Young Adults | FDIC.gov*, n.d.).

Let's talk benefits and risks. On the plus side, credit cards can be your best friend for building credit history. Having a good credit score can open doors, like getting loans for a car or a house without the bank laughing in your face. Many cards also come with rewards programs that offer cash back or points you can redeem for cool stuff. But tread carefully, because accumulating debt is as easy as getting sucked into a Netflix binge. One minute, you're swiping for a latte, and the next, you're contemplating selling a kidney to pay the bill.

Choosing the right card is cru- cial. Look for one with low in- terest rates, especially if you think you might not pay the full bal- ance monthly. No annual fees are a bonus, leaving you more cash for  things you actually enjoy. If you're into the perks, pick a card with re- wards that match your lifestyle—maybe travel miles if you're a jetset- ter, or cashback if you like a little something extra on your purchases. But remember, all that glitters isn't gold. Sometimes, those rewards come with caveats that make them less appealing. If there's an annual fee for the perks, maybe the free perks are actually imaginary. Not so perky after all, eh?

Case Study: Choosing Between Credit and Debit Cards

Imagine you're at a concert with friends, and everyone's buying merch. You pull out your debit card, knowing you can afford that band tee without stress. Your friend, however, reaches for a credit card. Why? They want the reward points for a future festival. This decision is fine *as long as* they plan to pay the full balance when the bill arrives. If they can't afford to do that, by the time that purchase has accumulated interest, that tee could end up costing more than a VIP ticket before it's paid off. This scenario shows the importance of understanding how and when to use each type of card, so you can rock out without financial regret.

In the end, both cards have their place in your wallet. Use a debit card when you want to stick to what you have, and reach for a credit card when you're confident in your payment plan. It's all about striking a balance, much like deciding between ordering pizza or cooking at home—each has its benefits, depending on the situation.

Smart Shopping and Avoiding Impulse Buys

Picture this: you're at the mall, casually strolling through the aisles when suddenly, out of nowhere, a wild sale sign appears. It's bright, alluring, and promises discounts that make your wallet tingle with excitement. Before you know it, you're at the checkout, buying a neon-green sweater that you'll probably wear—well—never. This, my friends, is the psychology of spending at work. Advertising techniques, emotional triggers, and even peer pressure can make us part with our hard-earned cash faster than you can say "buyer's remorse." Understanding these tactics helps you make smarter choices and dodge those sneaky impulse buys.

Marketers are like magicians, using clever tricks to make you want things you didn't even know you wanted. Ever notice how stores place the most tempting items at eye level? Or how they fill the air with delicious scents that make your stomach growl? These strategies are designed to tug at your emotional strings. Peer pressure adds another layer, especially when friends are flashing their latest purchases. It's easy to get swept up in the moment and make decisions based on fleeting emotions rather than logic.

So, how do you outsmart these crafty marketers and make informed purchasing decisions? Start by comparing prices. The internet is your best friend here. A quick online search can reveal if that awesome deal is actually as awesome as it seems. Reading reviews is another must. Real people sharing real experiences can save you from buying something that looks good in the store but falls apart after the first use. Here's a golden rule: wait 24 hours before making a purchase. This gives your brain a chance to catch up with your heart, ensuring you really want what you're about to buy. And if you're feeling really brave, consider paying with cash. Seeing those bills leave your hand can make spending feel more real, helping you think twice before splurging.

Budget-friendly shopping habits can also keep your spending in check. Coupons and discount codes are your allies—they're like little financial Easter eggs, just waiting for you to find them. Shopping during sales or in the off-season can also lead to big savings. And when it comes to essentials, buying in bulk can be a game-changer. You'll spend more upfront, but over time, you could save significantly on products you always need. Bulk isn't always guaranteed to equal savings, though, so here's a little trick. On the bottom of the price label on the shelf of most grocery stores, there will be a smaller price that tells you how much you are paying per unit. (Units could be pounds, ounces, pieces, etc.) For example, at Wal-Mart right now, I can spend $0.30 on one pack of Maruchan ramen noodles or $4.50 for a 12-pack of Maruchan ramen noodles. Before I decide whether the twelve pack is a better deal or not, I have two options: do some math, or look for the price per unit on the price tag. In this case, a quick look at the price tags and I learn that if I buy the single packs of ramen, I will spend 10 cents per ounce. If I buy the 12-pack, I will actually have to pay 12.5 cents per ounce. I could also figure this out myself by whipping out my calculator and dividing $4.50 (the cost of the 12-pack) by 12 to get the cost of each individual pack. This comes out to 37.5 cents per package, definitely more than the 30 cents per package if I buy them individually.

Thirty cents versus 37.5 cents may not seem like that big of a deal, but when you make the "not that big a deal" choice on every purchase you make over the next 10 years of grocery buying, you'll end up spending hundreds of dollars that you could have spent on a plane ticket to the  beach or a winter ski pass if you had just taken the time to quickly glance at the per unit price on the price tag to make sure you were getting the best deal.

Avoiding impulse buys is all about discipline and self-awareness. Make a shopping list and stick to it like glue. This list is your shield against unnecessary purchases. Set a spending limit before you hit the store and hold yourself accountable. Ask yourself if the item you're eyeing aligns with your financial goals. Do you really need it, or will it end up as closet clutter? Being mindful of these questions can help you resist those spur-of-the-moment temptations.

In the world of shopping, it's easy to feel like you're constantly being pulled in different directions. But with a bit of awareness and strategy, you can shop smartly and avoid those pesky impulse buys. It's about taking control of your spending habits and making decisions that are right for you, not just for the moment. So, next time you find yourself in front of a sale sign, take a deep breath, consider your options, and remember that smart shopping is about more than just saving money—it's about creating a lifestyle that works for you instead of against you.

Chapter 2

Culinary Confidence

I t's a Saturday afternoon, and your friends are all showing up for a taco party in a few hours. You could run to Chipotle and buy half a bathtub-full of tacos, but that'll cost you three times as much as if you prepped a homemade taco bar with ingredients from the local grocery store. Since you're following a budget now (wink, wink), you opt for the money-wise homemade route, but when you step into the kitchen with your bag of groceries to get started, you suddenly freeze. You've never cooked for anybody but yourself before. What were you thinking??

Don't worry. This chapter is your golden ticket to mastering the kitchen like a pro, minus the Gordon Ramsay-level yelling. By the time you're done, you'll have the confidence to whip up something delicious without setting off the smoke alarm even once.

Let's start with the essentials—the must-have kitchen tools that every aspiring cook needs. Now, when it comes to choosing the right tools, quality

matters. You don't need to break the bank, but investing in durable materials will save you from having to buy new tools all the time. Stainless steel is your go-to for knives and pans, offering longevity and versatility. And while hardwood cutting boards might be a bit pricier, they'll last longer than their plastic counterparts. If you're on a budget, look for restaurant supply stores—they often have quality tools for less. Or even better, scour your local thrift stores, estate sales, and yard sales. Sometimes you can find really good quality cookware for very cheap. Remember, a good set of kitchen tools is like a superhero team. Each one has its special powers, and together, they make you unstoppable in the kitchen.

First up is the chef's knife, your new best friend. This versatile tool can slice, dice, and chop whatever your culinary heart desires. It's all about precision and efficiency, turning you into a slicing ninja. I know if you look at a knife block in the store, you'll see twenty different knives in different sizes and shapes, but trust me, if you just invest in one good quality chef knife and a little practice, you'll be able to do anything and everything without ever looking back to wonder if you should have saved up for a year to buy the set of twenty knives.

Proper tool usage is crucial for safety and effectiveness. For knives, hold the handle firmly, with your fingers curled around it. Now scoot your hand forward and pinch the top of the base of the knife blade between your thumb and your curled index finger.

With your other hand, curve your fingers as if you were flexing bear claws and hold the food you are cutting with the tips of your fingers curved in slightly so that the middle section of your fingers create a vertical wall of sorts. This vertical wall is your defense against chopped fingers. Keep your hold-ing hand steady on the food, and begin chopping with a regular seesaw motion, leaving the tip of your knife on the cutting board while the rest of the knife moves up and down. (Obviously, depending on the size of the food you are cutting, this system might not always be possible, but if it is, use it!) This technique prevents accidents and gives you better control.

To keep your knives in top shape, maintenance is key. Sharpen your knives regularly to keep them slicing smoothly and store them properly in a knife block or on a magnetic strip. This not only prolongs their life but keeps your fingers safe from accidental cuts. Sharpening kitchen knives might sound intimidating, but it's not as tricky as it seems! The easiest way is to use a pull-through sharpener. Most have two slots, one marked "course" and one marked "fine" or something similar. Run your blade through the course slot first several times, forward and backward, and then finish by doing the same in the finer slot. Make sharpening your knives a regular habit—every week, or even every time you wash your knife. Don't wait until your knives are super dull—they're way harder (and more dangerous) to work with when blunt (Peterson, 2023)!

Quick Knife Skills Exercise

Try this: Grab an apple and practice your knife skills. Slice it into even wedges, focusing on your grip and control. See how thin you can make the slices without losing your fingers—bonus points if you can keep them uniform in size! This exercise builds confidence and precision. And who knows, maybe you'll discover a hidden talent for fruit art.

Other Important Tools

Next in line is the trusty cutting board. You want one made of hardwood—none of that flimsy plastic nonsense. It's your knife's partner in crime, providing a stable surface to work your magic. Bonus if you find one with a mini moat carved around the inside edge to catch the juices that try to run all over the countertop when you're cutting that especially ripe tomato. (It can also be helpful to find yourself two good cutting boards so that you can work on one with raw meat and the other with fruits and vegetables when you're prepping your meal, but if that's not in the budget, one good board that you wash thoroughly when switching between raw meat and other ingredients will work too.)

While wood cutting boards are more durable and longer-lasting than plastic, they will also require a little bit of extra attention. Over time and with repeated washings, wood will start to dry out. If your wood board gets really dry, it becomes susceptible to cracking. Wood is also porous, so as it loses its natural oils through washing, it gradually begins to absorb water and other liquids that it comes into contact with. In humid climates, this can lead to molding. To keep your board in top condition, when it starts to look dried out (one way to tell is that it will be much lighter in color than it used to be), get a bottle of food-safe mineral oil and a microfiber cloth. Make sure your board is clean and dry, then pour some mineral oil onto the surface and rub it in with your microfiber rag, front and back. Let it sit to absorb for a couple hours, and then wipe off any excess still on the surface before putting your cutting board to work again. You should do this about every month for best results, or more if your board is drying out quicker than that. Washing your wooden cutting board and any other wood cookware by hand with a simple dish soap (no abrasive chemicals) will help them last longer and need oiling less often.

Next up, don't forget the measuring cups and measuring spoons. Whether you're baking a cake or trying a new recipe, precise measurements are key. When using measuring cups, make sure to level off dry ingredients with a flat edge for accuracy. For liquids, bend down to eye level to ensure you're pouring the correct amount. These small details can make a big difference in your culinary creations. And, of course, mixing bowls are essential. If you find mixing bowls that come with fitting lids, then they're like the Swiss Army knife of the kitchen—use them for mixing, marinating, or storing leftovers.

Finally, find yourself one good flipping spatula, one good rubber spatula, a long-handled metal spoon, and a wooden spoon. With these four tools, you should be able to pull off anything you can imagine flipping, mixing, or stirring. Aim for a flipping spatula that is solid, not one with holes or grooves. It will be way easier to clean pancake batter and scrambled eggs off of. Rubber spatulas are perfect for mixing batters and making sure you get all the way into the corners of the bowl where the flour likes to cake, or scraping out the last bits of brownie batter into the baking pan. They are also what you will want to use if you have a pan with a non-stick surface, as metal spatulas will ruin the non-stick surface by scratching it up. Your two spoons will be as versatile as you make them. Stir sugar into your home-brewed sweet tea, reach down to the bottom of your pot of stew to give it a good mixing, or stir that mayonnaise into your macaroni salad. Similar to the rubber spatula, your wooden spoon is easier on any pans or dishware with delicate surfaces, whereas your metal spoon will do well with heavy duty stuff (Goldberg, 2016).

Before we move on from tool selection, I want to put a highlight on my personal all-time favorite kitchen tool: the cast iron skillet. They're tough as nails, so you never have to worry about which kind of spatula or spoon you're using. They hold and distribute heat evenly, so that you don't end up with your pancakes burned in the middle and still raw on the edges. They can be used on the stovetop *and* in the oven (skillet, baking dish, pie pan, and wok all in one). When maintained properly, they are also naturally non-stick! And if that's not enough to convince you, they also release small amounts of iron into your food when you cook in them. Wait! Before you freak out, that's actually a really good thing. According to the American Society of Hematology (that means blood scientists), as many as 40% of adolescents have an iron deficiency, which can lead to all kinds of problems, from simply having low energy levels to developing a serious medical condition called anemia (Whetzel, 2024). And cooking with cast iron pans has been proven to help supplement iron deficiencies (Sharma et al., 2021). If you want to learn more about that, check out the source websites referenced above and ask your family doctor more about iron deficiencies.

If you buy a new cast iron skillet (or a used one that hasn't been cared for well), you'll want to cure it before you start cooking with it. Curing (or seasoning) a new cast iron skillet is super simple and totally worth it because it gives the skillet that magical, non-stick surface everyone loves. Start by washing your new skillet with hot water and a little dish soap (it's the only time you should use soap on cast iron!) to remove any factory residue. Dry it completely—like, no moisture at all—because water and cast iron are not friends. You can even put it on the stove on low for a couple minutes to make sure all the moisture has evaporated out. Preheat your oven to about 450°F, rub a thin layer of vegetable oil, flaxseed oil, or another neutral oil all over the skillet (inside and out), and then bake it upside-down on the middle rack of your oven for an hour. Put a baking sheet below it to catch any drips. Turn off the oven, and let your skillet cool completely in the oven before taking it out (Lodge Cast Iron, 2023). Now your cast iron is ready for anything!

To clean your skillet after cooking, skip the soap. Washing it with soap will ruin the cure you've given it, take away its non-stick surface, and make your pan susceptible to rust. Use water and a scrub  brush or a chainmail scrubber to remove food bits. For stubborn stuck-on food, you can boil a little water in the skillet to loosen it up. Once it's clean, dry it completely, then rub on a super light coat of oil to keep the seasoning intact and protect against rust. Maintenance is key—avoid soaking it in water, and don't leave it wet. Treat it right, and your skillet will be your trusty kitchen buddy for life (Murray, 2023).

Finally, let's get familiar with your stove and oven. Whether you've got a gas, electric, or induction stove, each has its quirks. Gas stoves offer instant heat adjustments, while electric ones maintain a more consistent heat. Induction stoves, on the other hand, heat faster and are energy-efficient, but you have to use specific types of pans on

them because they create heat using magnetic energy. That means
your pans have to be stainless steel or iron because these metals have
magnetic properties. Your oven settings are equally important—broil
for a quick, intense heat from the top only (good for melting cheese
or toasting bread), bake for even cooking all around, and turn on the
convection setting if you want a faster, crispier result. Experiment with
these settings to find what works best for your dishes.

Simple and Nutritious Breakfasts

They say breakfast is the most important meal of the day, and let's be
honest, they're onto something. Imagine trying to tackle a full day of
school, sports, and socializing on an empty stomach. Not fun, right?
Plus, beginning the day with a meal jumpstarts your metabolism,
getting your body ready to burn energy instead of trying to conserve it
throughout the day. Starting your day with a nutritious breakfast fuels
your body and brain, giving you the energy and concentration you
need to ace that math test or charm your crush. A balanced breakfast
can lift your mood, improve performance, and prevent that dreaded
mid-morning slump when your brain feels like it's swimming through
oatmeal. So, let's transform your mornings with some easy, healthy
breakfast ideas.

Speaking of oatmeal, have you heard about overnight oats? They're
a game-changer for busy mornings. The night before, mix rolled
oats with your choice of milk or yogurt, and toss in some fruit and
nuts. Stick it in the fridge, and by morning, you've got a delicious,
ready-to-eat breakfast. No stove required! You can even drizzle some
honey or a sprinkle of sugar on top. If you're more of a smoothie person, try blending greens like spinach with fruits and a scoop of protein
powder or nut butter (peanut, almond, whatever you prefer). It's like

a superhero drink, packed with nutrients that'll keep you feeling full and focused. Or, if you're in the mood for something savory, whip up some avocado toast on whole-grain bread. Add a sprinkle of salt and pepper, maybe a poached or fried egg if you're feeling fancy, and you've got yourself a breakfast fit for a king. For a sweeter option, layer Greek yogurt with honey and granola. It's like having dessert for breakfast, minus the guilt. For a super healthy protein-packed option, whip up some loaded scrambled eggs. You can prep a container of chopped up veggies – like bell peppers, onions, tomatoes, spinach or whatever floats your boat – throw some chopped up ham and some shredded cheese in with it, and keep it in your fridge for the week. Each morning, you just have to scramble your eggs and grab a handful of your pre-chopped mix to throw into the skillet with them. Instant yum!

Now, let's talk about those days when you really can't be bothered to think about breakfast. Make-ahead options are your best friends here. Homemade granola bars are perfect for those grab-and-go mornings. You can customize them with your favorite nuts and dried fruits, and they're way better than anything you'll find in a vending machine. Another great option is egg muffins with veggies. Just whisk together some eggs, pour them into a muffin tin with your choice of vegetables, bake, and voila! You've got portable protein powerhouses ready to go. Check out the appendix for a step-by-step recipe for granola bars or egg muffins.

To keep breakfast exciting and prevent it from becoming a snooze-fest, mix things up with different ingredients. Experiment with seasonal fruits—strawberries in summer, apples in fall. Not only do they taste better when they're in season, but they're also often cheaper.

Try incorporating different types of whole grains like quinoa or barley into your morning routine. They're packed with fiber and will keep you full for longer.

Variety is the spice of life, and breakfast is no exception. With a little creativity, you can turn your morning meal into something you actually look forward to. Plus, starting your day on the right foot means you're more likely to make healthier choices throughout the day. So, whether you're a morning person or not, having a nutritious breakfast can set the tone for whatever challenges or adventures lie ahead (Melrose, 2024).

Simple Lunches and Dinners for Busy Days

Life is busy, and sometimes cooking feels like a chore that's best left to future-you. But with a dash of planning and a sprinkle of creativity, you can whip up delicious lunches and dinners that are both quick and satisfying. The secret is meal prepping. Think of it as a backstage pass to easier mealtimes. Spend a little time on the weekend chopping veggies, marinating proteins, or even pre-cooking grains. Store these ingredients in the fridge so that, when hunger strikes, you've got the makings of a meal ready to go. Time-saving cooking techniques, like using a slow cooker or an instant pot, can turn the culinary chaos into a manageable task also. These gadgets do the heavy lifting for you, allowing you to focus on more important things, like binge-watching your favorite show, hitting the court with your friends, or taking a hike through a fall forest.

For lunches that don't involve a sad desk salad of lettuce and croutons, con-sider chicken and veggie wraps. They're easy to make and incredibly versatile. Just

grab your favorite tortilla, spread some
hummus or your favorite sauce, and pile on grilled chicken with a
rainbow of veggies. Roll it up, slice it into pinwheels if you're feeling
fancy, and you've got a portable feast. Quinoa is another excellent option. Cook a batch of quinoa, toss it with cherry tomatoes, cucumber,
feta cheese, and a splash of lemon juice. You can throw in a chopped,
cooked chicken breast, sliced almonds, or cashews for a bigger protein
boost. It's refreshing, filling, packed with protein, and can be made
ahead of time. Plus, it's perfect for those days when the cafeteria line is
longer than a Monday morning. And I know I bashed on sad salads
at the beginning of the paragraph, but salads don't have to be sad!
Pick some dark, nutrient-dense leafy greens like spinach or kale instead
of just iceberg lettuce, top them with any of your favorite fruits and
veggies, some nuts, seeds, or cheeses for healthy fat, and a protein
source like sliced chicken breast or crumbled bacon for a nutritious
and delicious salad. (Pro tip: if you can include all the flavors of the
flavor star in your salad - or any dish you cook for that matter - it will be
way more exciting for your tongue. See if you can find ingredients to
incorporate sweet, savory, salty, sour, bitter, and spicy into your salad,
and notice how your once-sad desk salad is suddenly poppin'!)

When it comes to dinner, simplicity is your best friend. One-pot
pasta is a lifesaver, reducing both prep time and dishwashing agony.
Throw your pasta, sauce, and veggies into a pot, add enough water to
cover, and let it simmer until the pasta is al dente. Stir-fry is another
quick dinner hero. Use whatever protein you have on hand—chicken,
tofu, beef—toss it with a medley of vegetables, and serve over rice
or noodles. The beauty of stir-fry is in its adaptability; you can use
any veggies lurking in your fridge. Then there's the sheet pan dinner,
where you spread your choice of protein and vegetables across a baking
sheet, drizzle with olive oil, season with herbs, and roast until every-

thing is cooked to perfection. Less time in the kitchen, more time for everything else. Again, check out the appendix for some more detailed recipes.

"Now wait a minute, all this quick and easy stuff is fine and dandy, but what if I don't just want to live on quick and easy? What if I want to spice things up for a special occasion? Or impress a special someone with a little bit of gourmet? Or what if I just want to treat myself?"

I'm so glad you asked! Obviously there are a bazillion recipes online that you can follow to your heart's content, but if you don't want to always be a slave to recipes and you'd like to learn how to actually be *creative* in the kitchen, check out my other short book: *Cooking as Art: A Simple Guide to Creativity*. This short guide will teach you everything you need to know about flavor pairing, ingredient selection, color, texture, and more – all in simple language so that you can feel equipped to come up with your own creations in the kitchen and trouble-shoot recipes gone wrong with confidence.

Meal Planning on a Budget

Imagine you're standing in the middle of a grocery store, overwhelmed by endless aisles of choices. You went in for milk but somehow ended up with a cart full of Cheetos, bagels, and ice cream. Sound familiar? This is where meal planning swoops in like a caped hero, ready to save the day (and your wallet). By planning your meals in advance, you avoid the trap of impulsive grocery shopping. Having a detailed grocery list is like walking into the grocery store with the superpower of laser focus. Not only does this save money, but it also reduces food waste by ensuring you use up ingredients efficiently. Think of it as a puzzle, where each meal fits perfectly into the week, leaving no veggie behind to rot in the back of the fridge.

 Creating a meal plan is easier than deciphering a calculus problem. Start by listing your favorite meals—those go-to dishes you love and can whip up with your eyes closed. Now, mix in a few new recipes to keep things exciting. Balance is key, so aim for meals that include a healthy mix of proteins, carbs, veggies, and fats. As you plan, pay attention to food labels. Added sugars and trans fats are the villains here, lurking in processed foods and ready to hijack your healthy intentions. Shopping the perimeter of the store, where fresh produce, meats, and dairy reside, helps keep your cart filled with nutritious options. Use a meal planning template to organize your week. (There are lots of them for free online.) It's like having a roadmap, leading you to a week of delicious, stress-free dining.

Let's talk about shopping smartly and economically. As we mentioned in the first chapter, buying in bulk can sometimes be a fantastic way to save, especially for non-perishables like rice or canned goods. Just check that per unit price on the bottom of the price tag to make sure it's actually a better deal. You can portion and freeze bulk foods, ensuring they last longer and are ready when you need them. (Here's a few foods you might not think of that actually freeze really well and are just as good when defrosted later: bread, butter, cheeses, cooked rice, cooked pasta, tortillas, soup broths, chopped veggies, and herbs. Veggies and herbs are best used for cooking after they've been frozen, not so great for salads or fresh garnishes.) Buying fruits in season is another budget-friendly strategy. Not only are they cheaper, but they taste better too. Freeze them for smoothies or snacks later. And those store brands? Often just as good as the name brands but without the hefty price tag. Keep an eye out for sales and coupons, but remember, driving across town to save a nickel might cost more in gas than you save. Doing your shopping nearby can save gas money and require less time out of your day. Many grocery stores also now offer options to do all your shopping online and just drive by to pick it up, which can save even more time.

Batch cooking is your new best friend. When you cook large quantities at once, you've got meals ready to go throughout the week. Soups and stews are perfect candidates, filling your kitchen with comforting aromas and your freezer with future meals. Leftovers are not just yesterday's dinner—they're tomorrow's lunch. Roasted chicken can transform into chicken salad, and leftover veggies can add a nutritional punch to your morning omelet. It's a creative way to stretch your culinary efforts and your budget, turning one meal into many.

When you plan and shop with intention, you're not just saving money—you're crafting a lifestyle that's mindful and resourceful. It's about making choices that benefit your wallet, your health, and the planet. Meal planning on a budget isn't just a skill; it's a mindset that empowers you to navigate the culinary world with confidence and flair (*10 Tips for Planning Meals on a Budget - Unlock Food*, n.d.).

Try It Out: Quick Meal Prep Checklist

Develop a habit of jotting down your meal ideas at the beginning of the weekend and creating a prep checklist. What ingredients need chopping? Which proteins should be marinated? Make a list, and set aside a couple of hours to get it all done. This not only saves time during the week but also helps reduce food waste. Plus, there's something immensely satisfying about opening your fridge to see all those neatly prepped ingredients waiting to be turned into culinary masterpieces.

Busy days don't have to mean boring meals. These strategies and recipes are designed to make your life easier and your meals tastier.

With a little planning, you can enjoy home-cooked goodness without the stress, leaving more room for life's other adventures.

Cooking Safety and Hygiene

Now that the kitchen is your new playground, let's talk about the playground rules. Safety is your first ingredient for success. Start with the basics: keep those knives sharp. (I know, I know. We already talked about this, but let's just hammer it in, shall we?) A dull knife is more dangerous than a sharp one because it requires more force to cut, increasing the risk of slipping. When it comes to handling hot pots and pans, always use oven mitts or potholders. They're not just fashion accessories; they're your shield against burns. When transferring hot items, remain mindful of your surroundings and ensure that handles are not sticking out, waiting to catch an unsuspecting passerby.

Food safety is equally important, as nothing ruins a meal like a bout of food poisoning. Begin by washing your hands thoroughly before you even think about touching food. It's a simple step that can  prevent the spread of harmful bacteria. Proper storage of raw and cooked foods is crucial. Always store raw meat separately from other ingredients to avoid cross-contamination. Use airtight containers and refrigerate leftovers promptly. Cleaning and sanitizing countertops and cutting boards is non-negotiable. Use hot, soapy water when washing dishes. Remember, raw and cooked foods should never mingle on the same plate or cutting board – especially when working with meats! Keep them separated like feuding siblings at a family dinner (*Keep Food Safe! Food Safety Basics | Food Safety and Inspection Service*, n.d.).

Cooking temperatures matter, too. Invest in a food thermometer to ensure meats reach safe internal temperatures. Cook whole cuts of pork, like roasts and chops, to an internal temperature of 145°F and let them rest for three minutes after you remove them from heat before eating. Beef, veal, and lamb cuts allow for more variability depending on how you like to eat them: 135-145°F for medium, 145-155°F for medium-well, or 155+°F for well done. Ground meats are different, regardless of what they are made of, and should always be cooked to 160°F (this includes sausage patties and links). Poultry - chicken, turkey, cornish game hens, etc. - should always be cooked to 165°F, whether they are served whole or ground. Fish and shellfish should be cooked to 145°F (*Safe Minimum Internal Temperature Chart | Food Safety and Inspection Service*, 2020). When you temp your meat, do not remove it from the heat source while temping. Leave it in the oven or on the stove or grill, and stick your thermometer into the middle of the thickest part of your meat. Don't let the thermometer touch any bones, as bones hold heat differently than the meat does, and this will throw off your temperature reading. Leave the thermometer in place until the temperature stops changing and settles on a reading. If your meat is close to done (within 20 degrees of target temperature), you'll want to check again in 3 minutes or so. If it's not close, don't keep opening your oven or grill to check it again every few minutes, you'll just let all the heat out and make it take longer.

Even with the best precautions, kitchen mishaps can happen. Knowing how to respond effectively can turn a potential disaster into a minor hiccup. For minor cuts, apply pressure to stop the bleeding, clean the wound, and cover it with a bandage. If a minor burn occurs, run the affected area under cool water and avoid the temptation to apply ice, which can worsen the injury. In the event of a kitchen fire, *stay calm*. Smother small stovetop fires with a pot lid or drown them with baking soda. DO NOT USE WATER. Typically in kitchen fires, it's grease that catches on fire, and water can make grease fires explosive! A fire extinguisher is a kitchen must-have, and learning how to use it is just as important. For oven fires, turn off the heat and keep the oven door closed to smother the flames. If you can, unplug the oven or turn off the circuit breaker that gives it power until the fire is completely out and cleaned up. Do the same for toaster and microwave fires. Oxygen feeds fire, so keeping more oxygen from being introduced to the fire will keep it from growing. That's why you should always keep the door of your appliance closed if a fire starts inside it. If things get out of hand, don't hesitate to get help or call emergency services!

As we bring this chapter to a close, remember that culinary confidence isn't just about the food you make—it's about how you make it safely and hygienically, while creating an environment where you can cook confidently and enjoy the process. With these practices in your toolkit, you're not just preparing meals; you're laying the foundation for countless delicious experiences. Now you're ready to explore the vast and delicious world of cooking. Next up, we'll delve into the realm of health and wellness, where we'll look at how to fuel your body with the energy it needs to tackle whatever life throws at you.

Chapter 3

Holistic Health and Wellness

Exercise for Power Boosts

Have you ever found yourself huffing and puffing as you walked up the hill at your neighborhood park? Or maybe discovered that you're having trouble keeping up with your younger siblings or nieces and nephews when they want to play tag? Or even just found yourself in a pattern of having really low energy levels every day? That's where exercise can swoop in to save the day, turning you from couch potato to active dynamo. Exercise isn't just about sculpting those biceps or getting that six-pack; it's about feeling your best from the inside out. Regular physical activity is like a magic potion for your heart, improving cardiovascular health and keeping your ticker ticking. And let's not forget the mood-boosting endorphins that flood your brain after a good workout, leaving you grinning like a Cheshire cat. Exercise is also nature's sleep aid, helping you drift into dreamland faster than counting sheep. Plus, once you've made being physically active a regular part of your daily routine, you'll find your overall energy levels shooting through the roof.

So, what kinds of exercises should you include in your routine? Well, as we've said before, variety is the spice of life, and it's no different when it comes to fitness. Aerobic exercises are your go-to for getting that heart pumping and your lungs working like a well-oiled machine. Whether you're  running, cycling, swimming, or even dancing around your room, it's all about moving to the beat of your own drum to get your heart rate up and your lungs breathing deeper. The Department of Health and Human Services recommends getting at least 150 minutes of moderate aerobic activity or at least 75 minutes of vigorous aerobic activity a week (or a mix of moderate and vigorous). If you want to get really serious about aerobic exercise, you might consider using an online target heart rate calculator to help you figure out how many beats per minute (bpm) you want your heart at while you're exercising to get the most health benefits. This number is different for each person and takes into account factors like age, gender, and current physical health. Once you have that number, there are all kinds of fitness tracking devices that you can wear that will help you track your bpm live during a workout, or you can pause during your workout and measure your own pulse with your index and middle finger on your carotid artery (located in the top of your neck) or your radial artery (found on the wrist, near the base of the thumb). You can count your heart beats for 15 seconds and then multiply that number by 4 to get your approximate current bpm. If you don't want to be that technical, you can know if you're doing moderate aerobic exercise if you can have a conversation while you do it, but not sing. And if you're doing vigorous aerobic activity, you will only be able to say a few words at a time before having to pause to catch your breath. Again, this will be different for each individual. Don't worry about whether someone else thinks what you're doing is hard or easy! Just do what challenges your body and grows your personal heart and lung strength over time (*Exercise Intensity: How to measure it,* 2023).

Then there's strength training, which might sound intimidating, but trust me, it's nothing like lifting giant boulders. Bodyweight exercises like push-ups or squats are a great start, and resistance bands can add a little extra challenge. Flexibility exercises are the unsung heroes of fitness, keeping your muscles limber and reducing the risk of injury. Think mobility exercises or stretching routines that leave you feeling like a pretzel, but in a good way.

And let's not forget the fun stuff—recreational activities like sports, dance, kickboxing, or rock climbing. They're not just workouts; they're exercise disguised as play.

Creating a balanced exercise routine doesn't require a degree in rocket science. It's about setting realistic fitness goals that align with your lifestyle and interests. Start by deciding what you want to achieve. Maybe it's running a mile without collapsing or reaching a goal of 50 squats, or it could be a bigger goal like traveling to another state to run a really scenic marathon or climb an epic mountain. Once you've got your goals, mix in different types of workouts to keep things fresh and exciting. No one wants to do the same routine day in and day out—it's like eating plain oatmeal every morning. Also, allocate time for rest and recovery, because even super-athletes need a day off. Listen to your body and adjust your routine based on your progress and preferences. It's okay to swap running for cycling if that's what your body needs today. The key is consistency and making exercise a fun habit, not a chore.

Staying motivated and consistent can feel like climbing Mount Everest some days, but it's all about finding what works for you. Team up with a workout buddy or join a group, because exercising with others is like having your own cheer squad. Track your progress with a fitness journal or app to see how far you've come, and celebrate those wins, no matter how small. Reward yourself for meeting milestones—maybe with a new workout playlist or those trendy sneakers you've been eyeing. Music or podcasts can be your secret weapon, transforming a mundane workout into a jam session or a deep dive into your favorite topics. And avoid the temptation to measure your progress by comparing yourself to someone else! Everyone's body is different, and what it looks like to push your body to feel its best and have the most energy may not look anything like what it looks like for your friend to be healthy and in shape.

Try It Out: Personal Fitness Plan

Create your own fitness plan by jotting down your goals, preferred types of exercise, and a weekly schedule. Track your progress and adjust as needed. Celebrate each milestone with a small reward. Remember, this plan is yours, so make it fun and  tailored to your interests. Scan the QR code for more ideas about how to set up your fitness goals.

Exercise is your ticket to a healthier, happier you. It's not just about the physical benefits, but the mental and emotional ones too.

So lace up those sneakers, grab a friend or two, and hit the ground running—or dancing, or stretching! Whatever you choose, just keep moving forward.

Stress Management Techniques

Picture this: you're juggling school deadlines, trying to keep up with friends, and dealing with family drama—all while your phone buzzes with notifications demanding your attention. It's like a three-ring circus, and you're the main attraction. Welcome to stress, that sneaky little monster that loves to crash the party when things get over-whelming. It shows up in different costumes, sometimes as a headache that won't quit, muscle tension that feels like you've run a marathon, or even the emotional rollercoaster of anxiety and irritability. Left unchecked, stress can wreak havoc on your health, both physically and mentally, like an uninvited guest who never leaves.

 Understanding where stress comes from is like solving a mystery. Academic pressures are frequent suspects if you're still in school, with exams and assignments breathing down your neck. After school, work deadlines can step in to take over as stress inducers. Then there's the tangled web of social relationships, where drama can unfold faster than you can say "group chat." Family dynamics might add another layer, especially when everyone's under the same roof. Let's not forget extracurricular activities, which can feel like a balancing act worthy of the Olympics. Recognizing your own stressors is the first step to dealing with them, like shining a spotlight on the villain in a detective novel.

But fear not, because I'm here to arm you with strategies to outsmart stress. Breathing exercises can be your secret weapon, calming your body and mind like a gentle breeze on a hot day. If you feel your anxiety actively rising during a situation or conversation, take a time out and try deep breathing, where you inhale slowly through your nose, filling your lungs like a balloon, and then exhale through your mouth, letting all the tension float away. Diaphragmatic breathing is another technique, focusing on your diaphragm to take deeper breaths. Sit or lie down in a comfortable position with one hand on your chest and one hand on your belly. Breathe in through your nose so that your belly rises more than your chest does. Hold your breath for two seconds, and then exhale through your mouth. Do this for about 5 minutes. While you're doing breathing exercises, don't let your mind wander. Focus on your breaths and pay attention to how different parts of your body are feeling. Are there any parts of your body where you feel a lot of tension? If you're like me, you might hold stress in your neck and shoulders. While you breathe, focus on relaxing those muscles more and more every time you exhale. This allows your body to physically release stress from the places it is being stored. It's like hitting the reset button on your body's stress response (*Breathing Techniques for Stress Relief*, n.d.).

There's also something magical about physical activities like walking or stretching, which act as a release valve for pent-up stress. A stroll in the park or a few sun salutations can do wonders for your mood and mental clarity. Non-competitive cardio exercise is also one of the most effective ways to get rid of pent up cortisol. (Cortisol is a stress hormone that your body creates when it has experienced continual stress over long periods of time. Once it's created, there are very few ways to get it out of your system, but non-competitive cardio is one of them!) So go for a jog, a hike, or a bike ride and don't try to beat any times or reach any goals. Just get your heart pumping and sweat a little to release those toxins from your body.

Don't underestimate the power of sun-  shine, either. Spending time outdoors not only boosts your vitamin D levels but also helps regulate melatonin, which in turn aids in cellular healing. In Japan, they have a practice called "forest bathing," which involves spending time in nature to reduce stress and promote well-being. It's like a spa day for your soul, with the rustling leaves and chirping birds providing the perfect soundtrack. Creative outlets are another stress-buster, whether it's drawing, writing, or dabbling in watercolors. Letting your imagination run wild is a great way to express emotions and find joy in the little things.

And then there's classical music, the unsung hero of stress relief. Studies have shown that listening to classical music can reduce stress, enhance moods, and even improve cognitive functions like memory and focus (Des Moines Symphony, 2024). It's like a mental mas- sage, soothing frayed nerves and lulling you into a state of relaxation. Time management and organization can also be key players in the stress game, helping you stay on top of tasks and avoid the dreaded last-minute panic. We'll talk more on time management in the next chapter, but building non-negotiable rest time into your schedule is essential for healthy stress management.

Building a stress resilience toolkit is like crafting a superhero cape—ready to wear whenever stress strikes. Establishing a support network is crucial, whether it's friends who make you laugh, fam- ily who offer comfort, or counselors who provide guidance. Posi- tive self-talk and affirmations can be game-changers, reminding you of your strengths and abilities and addressing head-on any lies that have snuck their way into your thought life. Engaging in hobbies and leisure activities is another way to recharge, offering a break from the stressors of daily life. And remember, setting boundaries is essential to avoid over-commitment, because every hero needs time to recharge their batteries (Aacap, 2019).

With these strategies in your back pocket, you're better equipped to face stress head-on, turning it from an overwhelming foe into a manageable challenge. Embrace these techniques, adjust them to fit your personal needs, and build your resilience, knowing that you have the tools to navigate life's ups and downs with confidence.

Take the Next Step: Equip Your Stress Toolbox

Think about which of the strategies or activities mentioned above feels most helpful and realistic for you to incorporate into your weekly schedule. Is it breathing exercises? Walking? Zumba? Building a support network? Working on time-management and organization? Practicing saying "no" to overcommitting? Spending time in nature? Pick three of the tools discussed in the last section to be your go-to's for this month, and every time you start feeling stressed, intentionally practice one of those three stress management strategies. As you get comfortable with integrating those strategies into your life, you can add more strategies over time.

The Importance of Sleep and How to Improve It

You know the feeling. You're sitting in class, or in church, or at a work meeting, or at your grandma's dinner table, and you're doing everything you can to stay focused on the conversation, but your eyelids feel like they're being weighed down by invisible sandbags and your head keeps trying to roll around on the top of your neck. Sound familiar?

That's what happens when sleep decides to play hard to get. It's easy to underestimate the power of a good night's sleep, but trust me, it's like a secret potion that keeps you functioning at your best. Sleep is crucial for growth and development, especially during your teen years when your body is busy building and maintaining itself and your brain is experiencing major developmental growth.

Think of sleep as your personal construction crew, working overnight to repair and strengthen everything from muscles to memories. Skimping on sleep can leave you feeling foggy and forgetful, 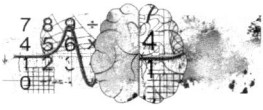 with the concentration of a goldfish, or worse. Trying to function without good sleep habits is like trying to run a marathon in the Mojave Desert with your shoes untied and no pants on—sure, it might be possible, but definitely not recommended.

But sleep does more than just power your body; it's a mood regulator, too. Ever noticed how everything seems a bit more dramatic when you're tired? That's because sleep helps balance your emotions by giving your brain the downtime it needs to process the day's events. Without it, you might find yourself crying over spilled milk—or worse, your favorite show getting canceled. Your immune system also benefits from a good rest, with sleep making way for the release of melatonin, which acts as your personal bodyguard, protecting you from illnesses and keeping you healthy by jumpstarting and regulating your body's immunity defense systems. So, if you want to dodge the sniffles and keep your mood in check, make sleep a priority.

Creating a sleep-friendly environment is like setting the stage for all of the adventures that await you in dreamland. Start by keeping your bedroom cool, dark, and quiet at night, turning it into a cozy cave where you can hibernate. A comfortable mattress and pillows are your best allies, supporting you like a loyal friend. Say goodbye to clutter and distractions that can mess with your zen, and consider using blackout curtains to keep unwanted light at bay. If noise is an issue, a white noise machine can be your lullaby, drowning out background sounds with soothing tones. The goal is to create a haven where sleep comes as naturally as breathing (Pacheco, 2024).

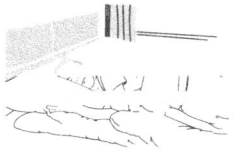 With your environment set, it's time to establish a bedtime routine that even the Sandman would envy. Start by setting a regular sleep schedule, going to bed and waking up at the same time each day, even on weekends. It's like training your body's internal clock, ensuring you wake up feeling refreshed and ready to tackle the day every time you wake. I know you might feel like on the weekend you deserve to treat yourself by staying up as late as you want and sleeping in as late as you want, but trust me, you deserve way better than that. You owe it to yourself to keep a regular sleep schedule so that you can wake up full of energy and mental clarity and enjoy every moment of daylight in your weekend instead of wasting it away laying in your bed. Give yourself a healthy sleep schedule; you deserve it! And you know what else you deserve? You deserve to not have a messed up circadian rhythm because of blue lights from screens. Your circadian rhythm is your body's internal clock that dictates everything from when you feel hungry, to when you feel productive and motivated, to when you go to the bathroom, to when you feel like it's time to fall asleep or wake up. All kinds of factors affect your circadian rhythm, and I highly recommend doing some of your own research to learn more about how it works. But I'll give you a freebee for now: blue light from screens is one of the

biggest culprits for messing up your body's natural circadian rhythm. When that blue light hits receptors in your eyes, it signals to your body that it's still daytime, and it won't let your body start producing melatonin. Melatonin is a hormone that is essential for our bodies to be able to enter sleep. If you are using screens in the last 2 hours before you try to go to bed, your body will not be able to fully enter sleep state because it will be blocked from creating melatonin (*Blue Light Has a Dark Side,* 2024). Look out for your body's needs! Make a pact with yourself to not use screens before bed. Instead, wind down with relaxing activities like reading a book or taking a warm bath. Avoid heavy meals and caffeine late in the day, as they can disrupt your sleep and leave you tossing and turning. (Caffeine can have delayed release in your bloodstream up to 12 hours after you consume it! Everyone's body is a little different, so pay attention to how caffeine affects you and adjust your intake routine accordingly.) Fight to create healthy rhythms for your body. You deserve to feel healthy and energized every day!

But what if sleep issues persist, like a pesky mosquito that won't leave you alone? In-somnia, the inability to fall asleep or stay asleep, can often be tackled with relaxation techniques. Try deep breathing exercises or progressive muscle relaxation to calm your mind and body. Finding a calming nighttime stretching routine can be helpful too. Sleep apnea, a condition where breathing is inter-rupted during sleep, might require medical advice and intervention. Restless legs syndrome, characterized by an uncontrollable urge to move your legs, can often be managed with lifestyle changes like reg-ular exercise and a balanced diet. Nightmares and night terrors can be daunting, but maintaining a consistent sleep routine and creating a safe, comforting environment can help reduce their frequency. And remember, what you feed your mind during the day is what it is digesting at night. Violence or horror in books, movies, or games are not helpful if you struggle with sleeping peacefully.

Sleep, in all its glory, is the unsung hero of health and wellness. It's the foundation upon which everything else is built, from your mental sharpness to your emotional resilience. As you prioritize sleep, you're setting yourself up for success in all areas of life. Now, as we drift towards the end of this chapter, remember that sleep is your ally, your companion on the journey to a healthier, happier you. With these tips in your toolkit, you're ready to embrace the night and wake up refreshed, ready to seize the day.

With sleep's mysteries unraveled, it's time to turn our attention to the next chapter where we'll explore the exciting realm of time management techniques. It's time to take ownership of your time.

Chapter 4

Time Management Techniques

It's Monday morning, and you've got a to-do list as long as a giraffe's neck. There's school, homework, soccer practice, a part-time job, your little sister's piano recital, and somehow you're supposed to find time to binge-watch the latest series everyone's talking about. It feels like you're juggling slippery

piranhas, and one wrong move could send everything crashing down. But what if I told you there's a secret weapon to tame the chaos? Enter the art of scheduling—your new best friend in the quest for balance and sanity.

Creating a weekly schedule might sound about as exciting as watching paint dry, but trust me, it's a game-changer. First off, it's a fantastic stress-buster. When you know exactly what's on your plate, there's less room for anxiety to creep in. Think of a schedule as your personal assistant, ensuring nothing slips through the cracks. It's like having a superpower that helps you prioritize what truly matters, from acing that history test to squeezing in some much needed downtime. Plus, ticking off tasks as you go brings a sense of accomplishment that's downright addictive.

Let's break down how to build this magical schedule. Start by listing all your commitments for the week—school, sports, chores, hangouts with friends. You name it, write it down. This gives you a bird's-eye view of your week and ensures you're not double-booking yourself like a Netflix special. Next, allocate specific time slots for each task. Be realistic; cramming an hour-long assignment into a 15-minute window is a recipe for disaster. Color-coding is your best ally here. Assign different colors to categories like school, work, and fun. It's like turning your schedule into a vibrant work of art, making it easy to spot what's coming up at a glance. Don't forget to pencil in breaks and leisure time. You're not a robot, and those pauses are crucial for recharging your batteries.

Now, let's talk tools. Gone are the days of scribbling on the back of your hand. Digital calendars like Google Calendar are fantastic for keeping everything in one place. They sync across devices, so you've got your 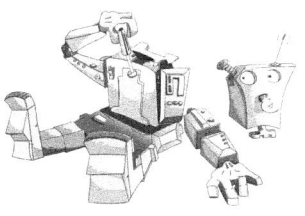 schedule at your fingertips wherever you go. If you're more of a tactile person, physical planners or bullet journals can be a helpful way to organize your life. There's something oddly satisfying about physically crossing off tasks. For you tech-savvy folks, planner apps like Todoist or Trello offer a modern twist with features like reminders and due dates. They're like having a personal assistant in your pocket, ready to keep you on track.

Of course, life loves throwing curveballs, and your schedule needs to be as flexible as a gymnast. That's why it's important to adjust it as needed. Maybe a surprise pop quiz means you need to shuffle study time, or a friend's spontaneous invite calls for a quick rearrangement. Flexibility in your time blocks is key. Don't plan something into every waking moment of your week. Leave some open spaces so that you can rearrange plans if someone asks you to reschedule an appointment or so that you can say yes to a spontaneous concert invitation without taking away time you need to study for your English test. Re-evaluate your priorities regularly to ensure you're focusing on what truly matters. And don't forget to communicate changes with others involved. A simple heads-up can prevent misunderstandings and keep everyone in the loop.

Get Your Hands Dirty: Weekly Schedule Template

Try creating your own weekly schedule using a template. List all your tasks and commitments, color-code them, and allocate specific time slots. Use this as a blueprint for your week. Adjust as needed and see how it feels to have everything mapped out. You might just find that scheduling becomes your new secret weapon for conquering the chaos. Check out the QR code for a suggested sample of how to manage your time:

 With the right approach, scheduling transforms from a mundane chore into a powerful tool for taking control of your time. It's like having a roadmap that guides you through the whirlwind of life, ensuring you're always on top of your game. Whether

you're juggling school, work, or just trying to find time for that all-important nap, a well-crafted schedule is your ticket to success.

Setting SMART Goals

Imagine you've got a dream, like tackling an alpine ice climbing route or acing that terrifying calculus exam. But dreams, as magical as they are, need a bit of structure to transform into reality. Enter SMART goals, your trusty blueprint for turning those dreams into achievable targets. SMART stands for Specific, Measurable, Achievable, Relevant, and Time-bound. Think of them as the ultimate checklist for goal-setting. Specific goals cut through the fog of ambiguity, providing clarity on what you want to achieve. Measurable goals give you a way to track progress, like leaving a trail of breadcrumbs to see how far you've come. Achievable goals keep you grounded, ensuring you're not setting yourself up for disappointment. Relevant goals align with your broader objectives, making sure you're climbing the right mountain. And Time-bound goals? They add urgency, setting deadlines that keep you moving forward (Ray, 2022).

Let's put SMART goals into action. Picture this: you want to boost your math grade from a B to an A by the end of the semester. That's Specific. You'll measure progress by tracking test scores and homework grades—Measurable. It's Achievable with some dedication and maybe a few

S	SPECIFIC
M	MEASURABLE
A	ACHIEVABLE
R	RELEVANT
T	TIME-BOUND

extra tutoring sessions. This goal is Relevant because it aligns with your desire to improve your overall academic performance. And by setting the deadline for the semester's end, it becomes Time-bound.

Or maybe you're a bookworm aiming to read one book per month for a year. This goal is Specific, Measurable, Achievable, Relevant to expanding your knowledge, and Time-bound with a monthly target. Fitness enthusiasts might aim to run a 5K race in under 30 minutes within three months. It's Specific, Measurable with your stopwatch, Achievable with training, Relevant to your fitness journey, and Time-bound with a clear deadline.

Achieving SMART goals isn't just about setting them; it's about the journey to get there. Start by breaking down your goal into bite-sized tasks. Each small victory builds momentum, like leveling up in a video game. Create a timeline for each task, so you're not overwhelmed by the final boss battle all at once. Let's take the last scenario above – running a 5k (3.1 miles) – and look at how that goal could be broken down:

- Weeks 1-2: Do two 100-meter sprints every other day to build strength, increasing speed by 5 seconds from original starting speed by the end of week 2.

- Weeks 3-4: Run one mile every other day, increasing speeds until I can run a mile in 15 minutes or less by the end of week 4.

- Weeks 5-6: Run 1.5 miles every other day, increasing speeds until I can run 1.5 miles in 30 minutes or less by the end of week 6.

- Weeks 7-8: Run 2 miles every other day, increasing speeds

until I can run 2 miles in 30 minutes or less by the end of week 8.

- Weeks 9-10: Run 3 miles every other day, increasing speeds until I can run 3 miles in 40 minutes or less by the end of week 10.

- Weeks 11-12: Run every other day, alternating between short runs (1.5 miles) and long runs (3.5 miles) each time I run. Aim to finish my short runs in 15 minutes or less by the end of week 12 and my long runs in 30 minutes or less by the end of week 12.

- Week 13: Run a 5k (3.1 miles) in 30 minutes or less!

You can develop a similar bite-sized goal method for any type of big goal that you are trying to achieve. Monitor your progress consistently, checking off milestones as you go. And remember, life isn't a straight line—adjustments are part of the process. Celebrate every achievement, no matter how small, because those moments of triumph fuel your motivation to keep going.

Of course, the path to success is littered with pitfalls, but fear not, for we shall navigate them together. One common mistake is setting goals as vague as a foggy day. Without clarity, you're like a ship without a compass, drifting aimlessly. Consider the two following example goals:

- I want to be a better swimmer.

- I want to be able to swim twice as many laps as I can swim now with the front crawl.

Which one of these goals gives me a clear target? Which one creates lots of opportunities to quit on days when I'm not feeling motivated because "technically I am a better swimmer than I was last week, most likely"?

Another pitfall is overcommitting. Setting too many goals at once is like trying to write a love sonnet while riding jet skis in a snowstorm. Focus on a couple significant goals to avoid burnout. Also, not tracking progress is a recipe for getting lost. Keep tabs on your journey to ensure you're heading in the right direction and keep yourself going by celebrating the small wins along the way. And finally, lacking motivation and accountability can be the silent saboteurs of your goals. Find a buddy to share your goals with or use apps to keep you on track.

SMART goals are your secret weapon for achieving greatness. They provide a roadmap to success, ensuring you're not just dreaming but doing. With clarity, structure, and a sprinkle of determination, there's no limit to what you can achieve. Whether you're aiming for academic excellence, personal growth, career advancement, or physical feats—Specific, Measurable, Achievable, Relevant, Time-bound goals are here to light the way.

Techniques for Beating Procrastination

Ah, procrastination—the sneaky gremlin that lurks in the shadows, waiting to pounce the moment you even think about starting something important. We all know it too well. You're supposed to be working on that essay, but somehow you've ended up watching cat videos or rearranging your sock drawer. Procrastination isn't just about being lazy. It's a psychological phenomenon that can stem from various sources, like fear of failure, perfectionism, or even just a plain lack of interest. These factors create a perfect storm that can stall productivity and ramp up stress levels, leaving you feeling like you're jamming down on the gas pedal but going nowhere.

To tackle procrastination, first, you need to understand your triggers. Maybe it's the fear of not doing something perfectly that holds you back. Perfectionism can paralyze you, making the task feel insurmountable. Perhaps it's the overwhelming nature of a project that makes you want to run for the hills, and you need it broken down into smaller pieces. Or, you might just find the task at hand as exciting as watching grass grow and lack the motivation to even start. Whatever your triggers are, identifying them is the first step towards overcoming them. Once you know what's causing you to procrastinate, you can start avoiding those triggers and working on strategies to beat procrastination (*Understanding and Overcoming Procrastination*, n.d.).

Speaking of strategies, let's talk about a few practical techniques to keep procrastination at bay. The Pomodoro Technique is a classic: work intensely for 25 minutes, then reward yourself with a 5-minute break. Repeat this cycle three more times, and then take a longer 15-30 minute break (Raeburn, 2024). Use a timer to keep track, and watch your productivity and focus soar with this technique. It's like a game, racing against the clock and rewarding yourself with a break. Time blocking and setting deadlines can also help. Allocate specific time slots for tasks, creating a sense of urgency that can boost focus. Prioritizing tasks using the Eisenhower Matrix (Team Asana, 2025), which divides tasks into urgent and important categories, helps you focus on what really matters. (See more details on that in a moment.) There are also lots of different apps designed to help you manage time and prioritize tasks (Haydon, 2024). Just make sure that you're not researching time management apps as another way to procrastinate doing what you actually need to do! Creating a distraction-free environment is crucial, too. Clear your workspace of clutter, *turn off notifications*, and give your brain the peace it needs to concentrate.

Building long-term habits to combat procrastination is like training for a marathon. It takes time and consistency. Establishing a daily routine helps structure your day, reducing decision fatigue. The more predictable your schedule, the less likely you are to procrastinate. Practicing self-discipline and self-control is key. Set small goals and reward yourself when you stick to them, reinforcing positive behavior. And don't forget about the power of accountability. Share your goals with friends or family who can support you and keep you on track. Sometimes, a little external pressure is what you need to stay focused.

With these strategies, you can transform procrastination from a formidable foe into a tamed tiger. You can start understanding your habits, find what works for you, and create an environment where productivity can flourish.

Balancing School, Work, and Social Life

Imagine trying to ride a unicycle while juggling. Now add a flaming torch to the mix, and you've got a pretty good idea of what balancing school, work, and social life feels like. Yet, mastering this balance is crucial for your well-being. Without it, burnout and stress can creep in, leaving you feeling like a deflated balloon. But when you find that sweet spot, you're not just surviving—you're thriving. It boosts your productivity and satisfaction, making those endless to-do lists feel less like chores and more like stepping stones to success. Plus, a balanced life enhances your relationships and social connections, reinforcing your support network and promoting both mental and physical health. It's like finding the cheat code to a happier, healthier you.

So how do you prioritize these commitments without feeling like you're being pulled in a million directions? Start with a priority matrix. A well-known version is the Eisenhower Matrix that we mentioned briefly earlier. Picture a grid with two axes: urgent to non-urgent and important to non-important. In this system, "urgent" refers to whether or not something has a time deadline that's coming up soon. "Important" refers to whether something is personally important to you in order for you to reach your life's big-picture goals.

	Urgent	Not Urgent
IMPORTANT	**Do It:** 1. Critical school work 2. Paying bills 3. Critical medical 4. Critical car repairs	**Schedule it:** 1. Exercise 2. Relationships 3. Car maintenance 4. House maintenance 5. Meal prep & cooking 6. Self improvement
NOT IMPORTANT	**Delegate:** 1. Favors 2. Some emails 3. Unscheduled calls 4. Shopping (sales) 5. Errands	**Delete:** 1. Social media 2. Web browsing 3. Video games 4. TV 5. Some undesired social "obligations' that could be avoided with boundaries.

Often, we spend most of our time on things that are urgent, but not actually important to us. The goal is to put time-management and scheduling techniques in place that help us spend most of our time working on things that are important to us personally, ideally without them having to become urgent before we do. This tool helps you identify what needs immediate attention and what can wait. School assignments and work shifts often fall into the urgent and important category, and recognizing these non-negotiables helps you allocate time effectively. But remember, it's not all about work. Allocating time for social activities and hobbies is equally important. They're not just add-ons; they're integral to maintaining balance and sanity. It's like building a playlist with both upbeat and chill tracks, keeping you energized and relaxed.

Now, let's talk time management strategies that can make this balancing act a little less daunting. Learn to set boundaries and don't be afraid to say no. It's tempting to say yes to every invite or opportunity, but overcommitting can lead to exhaustion. If you struggle with overcommitting yourself, sit down at the beginning of the week and decide ahead of time how many "yeses" you realistically have capacity for this week. If you have time in your schedule for two yeses this week, then once you have said yes to two extra activities for the week, all other invites receive a "sorry, not this time." Decide on your number at the beginning of the week, and don't let yourself compromise. You're guarding your mental health and sanity here – don't let peer pressure steal that from you. Combining activities is another clever trick. Consider joining a study group with friends. You get the best of both worlds—studying and socializing in one go. And don't underestimate the power of downtime. Use your commute or breaks to catch up on reading or plan your day. Technology is your ally, too. Set reminders and alerts on your phone to keep you on track without the mental clutter. It's like having a personal assistant who doesn't demand coffee breaks.

While you're juggling these commitments, don't forget about self-care and relaxation. These aren't luxuries; they're necessities for maintaining balance. Schedule regular breaks and leisure time, even if it's just a few minutes to unplug from electronic devices and relax.

"What? Did she just say I should not use electronic devices while I relax??" **Yes.** *Here's a newsflash for you, time spent in front of screens does*

not count as relax time because those activities actually stimulate your brain and are proven to increase stress levels. Time in front of screens "overloads the sensory system, fractures attention, and depletes mental reserves," leaving your brain more drained than when you started (What does screen time do to my brain? | SUNY Potsdam, *2025*). *Ouch. That sounds like the opposite of relaxing...*

Engage in activities that actually promote relaxation, like reading a captivating book (not on a screen), doing something creative, or spending time in nature. Practicing mindfulness and stress-relief techniques can also be beneficial. They're like a reset button for your mind, helping you recharge and refocus. And, of course, ensure you're getting enough sleep and exercise. A well-rested and active body is better equipped to handle life's challenges.

Balancing different aspects of life isn't just about keeping your head above water—it's about enjoying the swim. When you prioritize commitments, manage your time effectively, and embrace self-care, you're setting yourself up for success. It's all about creating a lifestyle where you're  in control, not overwhelmed. With these strategies, you're not just surviving the chaos; you're thriving in it.

As we wrap up this chapter, take a moment to appreciate the power of balance. It's the secret ingredient to a fulfilling life, where you're not just checking off tasks but savoring each moment. Up next, we'll explore the world of household maintenance, because a well-balanced life also means knowing your way around a toilet brush and a screwdriver.

Chapter 5

Household Maintenance Basics

Your home is supposed to be that safe sanctuary you can enter to get away from the chaos of the world. But what if stepping into your house actually feels like stepping straight into the mouth of chaos itself? Where are you supposed to go then? I don't want that to be your story, so let's take a look at some useful skills to help keep your home a place that feels restful, manageable, and safe.

Doing Laundry Like a Pro

Once upon a time, in a land of mismatched socks and mysterious stains, I faced an epic battle against the dreaded laundry monster. It was a beast of tangled clothes, cryptic labels, and endless cycles. I remember standing in front of the washing machine, bewildered by the knobs and buttons, with a pile of clothes that seemed to mock my every move. That was the day I vowed to conquer the chaos and become a laundry pro. So grab your detergent, because it's time to turn the laundry room into your personal battleground.

Let's start with the basics. Under-standing laundry is like mastering a new language. It begins with sorting your clothes, which is more about avoiding a wardrobe disaster than anything else. Separate your laundry by color: whites, darks, and colors that scream for atten-tion. Fabrics matter too. Group delicate fabrics like silk or lace together, and keep those heavy-duty jeans away from your softest tees. Then, there's the care label—a tiny tag that holds the secrets to your clothes' survival. It's your laundry Rosetta Stone, re-vealing washing temperatures, drying instructions, and other arcane symbols. Don't ignore it, or you might find your favorite sweater transformed into a doll-sized disaster. Finally, keep heavily soiled items apart. Mixing them with lightly worn clothes is like inviting a mud wrestling match into your washing machine.

Now that you've sorted through the chaos, it's time to tackle the laundry process step-by-step. Loading the washing machine might seem straightforward, but there's an art to it. Don't cram everything in like you do with your suitcase for vacation. Clothes need space to dance around and get properly cleaned. Choose the right deter-gent—an all-purpose one with enzymes is usually a safe bet, but follow the instructions for the right amount. Overloading on detergent can leave your clothes with a soapy residue, while too little might not get them clean enough. Select the appropriate wash cycle and tempera-ture: cold water for most clothes, hot for towels and sheets. Gentle cycles are for those delicate fabrics that need a little extra TLC. If you're using fabric softeners or bleach, add them at the right time and in the right spot based on your washing machine's instructions, but remember, they're not always necessary. Bleach is powerful, so use it sparingly to avoid mishaps (Leverette, 2024).

Once the washing is done, it's time to dry and fold like a pro. You have two choices: air drying or using a dryer. Air drying is gentle and energy-efficient, but it takes longer. If you opt for the dryer, avoid overloading it, or you'll end up with a tangled mass that resembles the Gordian knot of ancient Greek legend and dry times longer than the last class period of the day.

Empty your dryer's lint trap after every use and clean the dryer vents regularly to avoid a fire hazard—trust me, a surprise fire drill isn't on anyone's to-do list unless you're a school principal. To clean the lint trap, just pull out the screen that catches  lint, usually found somewhere on the top or front of your dryer, depending on the model you have. Use your hand to swipe any lint off the screen and throw it in the trash, and then slide the screen right back in where you found it. Cleaning out your dryer vent yourself is pretty straightforward and super important. First, unplug the dryer (safety first!) and pull it away from the wall so you can get to the vent. Disconnect the vent hose (it's usually a big, flexible tube held on with simple snap clamps) from the back of the dryer and the wall connection. Use a vacuum with a hose attachment to suck out lint from both ends of the vent. If the vent is super clogged, grab a dryer vent cleaning kit from your local hardware store—those have long brushes that can reach farther inside (Consumer Reports, 2023). Check the vent's exit on the outside of your house also—make sure it's not blocked by lint or debris. Once it's all clean, reattach the hose, push the dryer back, and plug it in. Easy peasy, and you should do this every 6–12 months (U.S. Fire Administration, 2023).

 When it comes to folding laundry, each type of clothing has its rhythm, but there is definitely more than one way to do it. The important thing is, don't just wad clothes up if you don't want them to be a wrinkled mess later—fold in straight lines. Delicate items deserve hangers to maintain their shape. If you forgot to get your clothes out of the dryer in time and discover when you get to them that all your T-shirts have settled into wrinkled patterns more grotesque than a shriveled raisin, just throw them back in the dryer with a damp washcloth for 10 minutes or so to loosen them all back up again, and then remove them promptly and fold them immediately for a wrinkle-free wardrobe.

But what about those pesky laundry issues that seem to pop up at the worst times? Discovering a stain is like discovering a new wart in a less than conspicuous location, but they can be tackled effectively. Use stain removers or pre-treat stains by rubbing a bit of detergent on them before washing. For stubborn blood stains, cover the stain with some hydrogen peroxide and let it sit for five minutes before washing normally, or make a mixture of two parts water to one part white vinegar and soak your clothing item in it for 10-20 minutes before washing normally. For oil stains, put baking soda or cornstarch on the stain to soak up the oil if it's a fresh stain. If it's already set in the fabric, a grease fighting dish soap, such as Dawn, can be really helpful. Scrub it into the affected area with a toothbrush, then wash the garment normally with warm water to help finish loosening up the grease. For color bleeding accidents, oxygen bleach can save the day. Just follow the directions on the container for proper use. If clothes shrink, try soaking them in a mixture of water and baby shampoo to relax the fibers. Stretching them gently can help restore their shape. On the flip side, if something stretches, a warm wash and a tumble in the dryer can sometimes shrink it back (Leverette, 2024).

Let's Review: Laundry Care Checklist

Here's a quick checklist for your next laundry day:

- Sort clothes by color and fabric type.

- Check care labels for special instructions.

- Use the right amount of detergent and select the appropriate cycle.

- Choose between air drying or using the dryer.

- Fold and hang clothes promptly to keep them wrinkle-free.

This can feel like a lot of steps, but if you set yourself up with a weekly or bi-weekly laundry routine that is planned into your schedule, it will help you fight off procrastination goblins. Keep in mind that you don't have to wash every clothing item after just one use either. If it doesn't smell and didn't have any spill mishaps, throw it back in your drawer to wear again instead of into the laundry bin. This not only saves you time, but keeps your clothes from wearing out as quickly, since fabric fibers degrade a little bit every time you wash them (Leverette, 2024). You can also turn laundry day into a fun event by playing your favorite tunes or listening to a podcast while you sort laundry and rewarding yourself with watching Netflix while you fold your clothes at the end of the process. With these tips, you'll conquer the laundry monster and emerge victorious.

Keeping Your Space Clean and Organized

Ah, the mysterious case of the vanishing socks and the untamed chaos of your living space. We've all been there, staring at a room that looks like a tornado went through it. But fear not, because maintaining a clean and organized space can be surprisingly simple with a few daily habits (emphasis on *daily* here—when messes are left to the element of time, they grow exponentially...). Start by making your bed every morning. It's a small task that can set the tone for the day, giving you a sense of accomplishment right out of the gate. Plus, it makes your room look instantly more put together. A quick sweep or vacuum of high-traffic areas prevents dirt from building up. Putting things back in their designated spots immediately instead of letting piles grow on floors, countertops, or beds gives everything a home, reducing clutter and stress and making cleaning days a much simpler project. Wash dishes or load them in the dish washer immediately after each meal. Think of these daily habits as a gift to future-you so that future-you doesn't collapse into a state of overwhelmed panic a month from now when your room and the entire house qualify as a natural disaster, warranting hazmat suits and a full 24 hours of dedicated scrubbing and organizing. Trust me, a little bit of effort every day is way better than trying to muster the motivation to do a complete overhaul every few months.

For those tasks that don't need daily attention, a weekly or monthly schedule can work wonders. Dedicate a day each week to dusting and vacuuming the entire house. Not only does this keep allergies in check, but it also gives everything a clean slate. Bathrooms, often the battlegrounds of grime, deserve a thorough cleaning. Scrub toilets, sinks, and showers with an antibacterial bathroom cleaner to prevent any unwelcome surprises. And don't forget about windows and mirrors. A glass cleaning spray and a little elbow grease can make them sparkle and add vibrancy to your space. Closets and drawers also crave attention. Decluttering and organizing them monthly helps keep your belongings accessible and your space serene. For a look at a sample cleaning schedule, scan the QR code:

 Let's talk more about keeping things organized, because a clutter-free space is a happy space. Storage bins and baskets are your allies, hiding away items that don't need to be on display. Labeling containers is a game-changer, especially when you're in a rush and need to find something quickly. Utilizing vertical space with shelves and hooks can transform your room, giving you more storage without taking up precious floor space. And here's a golden rule: the "one in, one out" strategy. For every new item you bring in, say goodbye to something old. It's a nifty trick to avoid clutter and keep your space feeling open and welcoming.

When it comes to cleaning supplies, having the right tools makes all the difference. An all-purpose cleaner and disinfectant are must-haves for tackling a range of surfaces. Read the directions on the bottle for best use practices. Dry microfiber cloths are great for polishing metal and glass surfaces to a sparkle after they've been cleaned with a glass cleaner and regular rag. Sponges with an abrasive surface on one side are perfect for cleaning soap grime build-up out of bathtubs and showers or scrubbing the "whoops, I missed" spots around the base of the toilet. A broom, mop, and vacuum cleaner form the holy trinity of floor care, ensuring no crumb goes unpunished. A dedicated toilet cleaner (not just the all-purpose cleaner you use everywhere else) and toilet brush are essential for bathroom maintenance, keeping everything hygienic and fresh. (Do you recall our toilet brush story from the beginning of our book journey? Don't let that be you; get familiar with the art of scrubbing your toilet out with a toilet brush.) With these tools in your arsenal, you're well-equipped to handle whatever mess life throws your way.

As you embark on this tidy adventure, remember that cleaning isn't just about making things look nice. It's about creating a space where you can relax, focus, and thrive. A tidy environment fosters a tidy mind, and with these tips in hand, you're ready to transform your space into a haven of organization and cleanliness.

Basic Home Repairs Everyone Should Know

Ever turned off a faucet only to be serenaded by the incessant drip, drip, drip of a leaky tap? It's nature's way of testing your patience and water bill. Fixing a leaky faucet isn't just a rite of passage; it's an opportunity to channel your inner handyman. First, locate the water supply valve under the sink and turn it off. There may be two valves, one for hot and one for cold, in which case they will both need to be turned off. (For most pipes, if the valve handle is parallel to the pipe, the valve is open; if it is perpendicular to the pipe, the valve is closed.) No one wants an impromptu indoor water park. Once the water is off, carefully disassemble the faucet. It will be a good idea to use your phone and take pictures of the parts you take off at each step and where they were attached so that you can reference them when you put it back together later if you need to. You might need a wrench or screwdriver, depending on the faucet type. Look for worn-out washers or O-rings, which are often the culprits of leaks. Replace them with new ones—these small rings are the unsung heroes of leak prevention. You can purchase new ones at any hardware store. Take your old one to match the size and shape when you buy the new one. Don't be afraid to ask employees at the hardware store for help finding an exact match. They can save you a lot of time wandering up and down aisles. Reassemble the faucet and test it by turning the water back on. If the drip has vanished, congrats, you've just leveled up in home maintenance!

Clogged drains are every sink and shower's worst nightmare (not to mention the dreaded toilet clog). You may have been there before—ankle-deep in water during a shower, feeling like you're on the brink of a plumbing apocalypse. Fret not, because unclogging drains is simpler than it sounds. Start by removing the drain cover and looking with a flashlight to see if there are any obvious obstructions in the drain. In a shower, a common culprit is hair built up in the drain, and you may just be able to reach in and clean it out with your hand. (Wear a rubber glove if touching slimy hair isn't your jam.) If there is no obvious culprit once you've removed the drain cover, start with a plunger, your first line of defense. Position it over the drain and push down firmly, creating a seal. The goal is to use suction to dislodge whatever is causing the clog. Pull the plunger up and down at regular intervals for several minutes, forcing air in and out of your drain to dislodge whatever is stuck. If the plunger doesn't do the trick, a drain snake might be your next attack plan. Insert it into the drain and twist until it grabs the blockage, then carefully pull

it back out, culprit in hand. Avoid chemical drain cleaners as much as possible, as they can damage pipes. If you feel the irresistible urge to use chemical drain cleaners, be sure to read the directions carefully and follow all safety precautions. They are very potent and dangerous chemicals. If all else fails, a plumber might be in your future, but at least you've given it your best shot.

Walls are like blank canvases that sometimes end up with holes, courtesy of nails, accidents, or an overenthusiastic game of indoor basketball. Repairing these blemishes is a skill worth having. Begin by cleaning the area around the hole, removing any debris or loose paint. Apply spackling paste for small holes or use a wall patch kit to fill a bigger hole, smoothing it out with a putty knife. (All these supplies can be found at your local hardware store. Again, don't be afraid to ask employees for help to find what you need and to explain the different options to you. Also, watching a YouTube video about how to patch a hole in the wall can be very helpful alongside the instructions on the patch kit.) Whichever system you use, once it has dried long enough according to the product directions, sand the surface using a fine grade sandpaper until it's smooth and even. If the rest of the wall is textured, buy a can of spray texture and follow the instructions to texture the repair before painting. Match the wall color with a fresh coat of paint, and voilà, it's like the hole never existed. Not only does this fix improve aesthetics, but it also keeps the wall structurally sound, saving you from further issues down the line (Digital, 2023).

Let's talk about light bulbs and batteries. They're the unsung heroes of household illumination and power, yet they often go unnoticed until they burn out or die. Choosing the right type of light bulb is crucial. LEDs are energy-efficient and long-lasting, while CFLs offer a good balance of efficiency and brightness. Safely replacing bulbs involves turning off the switch connected to the bulb and using a sturdy step stool to reach the fixture. Gently remove the old bulb and replace it with the new one, ensuring it's screwed in securely. It's important to make sure that you replace the bulb with a new bulb of the same wattage. Look at the old bulb or at the tag inside your light fixture to see what wattage of bulb to purchase for a replacement. Most typical light fixtures use 60-watt bulbs, but again, check your specific fixture. (The recommended wattage is what that fixture can safely support, so don't ignore that number.) When it comes to smoke detectors, carbon monoxide detectors, and remote controls, battery replacement is key. Test smoke and carbon monoxide detectors monthly by pushing the "test" button to make sure they are working. Always have a variety of batteries on hand, and when replacing them, check for leaks. If your batteries have leaked, you'll see a white, blue, or greenish powdery substance on the metal parts in your battery terminal. You'll need to clean any corrosion from the terminals to ensure proper contact when you put new batteries in. Wet a cotton swab with white vinegar or lemon juice and apply it everywhere you see signs of corrosion to neutralize the battery acid. Let it sit for a minute, then wipe it out with a microfiber cloth or lint-free rag. Make sure the battery compartment is completely dry before putting any new batteries in.

Loose screws are sneaky little things. They start as a minor annoyance and can quickly become a major headache if ignored. Whether it's a wobbly door handle, a swaying chair, or a dresser knob that just won't stay put, tightening screws is a simple fix. Find the offending screw, grab a screwdriver with a tip that matches the screw-head, and turn clockwise until it's snug. Don't over-tighten, as it could strip the screw or damage the material. It's a small task, but one that can save you a lot of trouble in the long run.

 Now on to the yard. If it's your first time tackling yard work, don't sweat it—you'll get the hang of it fast! First up is learning how to use and maintain a lawn mower and weed whacker. For the mower, check the gas and oil levels before you start. If you need to refill gas or top-off oil, reference your owner's manual for types of gas and oil.

Push or ride in straight lines, overlapping a bit so you don't miss spots. After mowing, clean off the grass clippings stuck under the mower to prevent rust (Consumer Reports, 2023). With a weed whacker (or string trimmer), start it up and carefully trim along edges of sidewalks, flower beds, or fences – anywhere your lawnmower can't reach. Keep the string close to the ground but not so low that you hit dirt and wear out the string too fast. If the string breaks, you'll have to turn off the weed whacker and unwind some more from the spool before you keep going. After using any tools, clean them off and store them in a dry place—they'll last way longer that way.

If you live somewhere where you experience a cold winter and won't need to be mowing for several months during the winter, make sure to either empty all the fuel from the tank of your mower (and weed whacker if it's not electric), or add fuel stabilizer to the fuel tank and run the engine to circulate the stabilizer through it before leaving it to sit for the winter. If you don't add stabilizer or empty out the fuel, the gasoline will start to break down while your mower is sitting and leave gummy deposits that will clog up your engine and carburetor and make starting up your mower again in the spring a much more complicated ordeal.

Beyond mowing and whacking, keeping your yard looking good is all about weed control and watering. Pull weeds regularly or use a pre-emergent weed killer in the spring to stop them from growing in the first place (HGTV, 2023). For watering, aim to do it early in the morning—your plants will soak up the water before the sun gets too intense, and you'll avoid fungus issues. Lawns generally need about 1 inch of water per week, which you can track with a simple rain gauge; however, your climate will make your lawn's specific needs unique. Moreover, some states have water-use restrictions in place because of droughts. Do a little research to find out how much water lawns in your specific area should need. For gardens, water the base of plants instead of spraying the leaves, and check the soil—if it feels dry a couple of inches down, it's time to water. If the soil is still damp, hold off on watering for another day. Overwatering can be just as dangerous for plants as underwatering and makes them susceptible to bacterial growth and infections. Start with these basics, and you'll have a healthy yard in no time!

These basic home repairs and maintenance tasks might seem daunting at first, but with practice, they become second nature. Embrace the challenge and enjoy the satisfaction of fixing things and maintaining your yard yourself. Your home will thank you!

Understanding Utility Bills and How to Reduce Them

You open your mailbox, and there it is—the dreaded utility bill. It's like a letter from a mysterious pen pal who only ever wants to talk about money. But fear not! Deciphering these bills can be easier than it seems. Here's a sample utility bill with each section labeled for you:

 Start by breaking down the components. Utility bills usually include usage, rates, and fees. Usage tells you how much electricity, water, or gas you've gulped down that month. Rates show how much you're paying per unit of each utility used, and fees

cover extra charges like service fees or taxes. Keep an eye out for patterns in your usage. If your bill skyrockets every summer, it might
be your overzealous air conditioner to blame. Comparing past bills is
like playing detective, helping you spot trends and changes that might
need attention. To reduce air conditioner usage, open your windows
overnight when it's cooler, and close them as soon as the sun is up
during the day to lock the cool night air in. Also keep blinds and curtains closed during the day to keep the sun out and keep temperatures
cooler. To reduce heat usage in the winters, set your thermostat lower
and wear sweaters and socks around the house. Snuggly, comfy clothes
create the perfect winter vibes anyway. It's like a warm hug that saves
money.

Speaking of saving money, here's some energy-saving tips that can
make a world of difference in reducing those bills. Start by turning
off lights and appliances when they're not in use. Energy-efficient
light bulbs and appliances are your allies here, using less power to do
the same job. LED bulbs, for example, are a bright idea—they use
a fraction of the energy compared to traditional bulbs. And don't
forget about phantom energy drain—unplug electronic devices like
computers, game consoles, and battery chargers when not in use to
prevent them from silently sipping electricity (Morris, 2024).

Water conservation is another key player in the quest to conquer
utility bills. Fixing leaks promptly is a must. A dripping tap might not
seem like a big deal, but those drops add up. Low-flow showerheads
and faucets are a smart investment, reducing water usage without
sacrificing pressure. Taking shorter showers is an easy way to save.
Think of it as a race against the clock—how fast can you lather up
and rinse off? Collecting rainwater for outdoor use is a nifty trick,
especially if you're a fan of gardening. It's like nature's free refills for

your plants. (Some states have laws about this, so do some research about your state's laws before you set out any rain barrels.)

Budgeting for utilities is all about planning ahead to avoid surprises. Set aside a portion of your income for utilities each month, just like you would for rent or groceries. Many utility companies offer budget billing plans, which spread your costs evenly throughout the year instead of your costs fluctuating significantly each month based on usage. This can keep you from getting your socks blown off when those summer air conditioning bills try to knock you over. Monitoring your usage regularly helps you stay within budget. It's like having a crystal ball that shows you where your money is going so you can make adjustments as needed.

As we wrap up this chapter on household maintenance, think of these tips as tools in your belt, ready to tackle the everyday challenges of managing a home. From understanding utility bills to home repairs, yard care, and laundry day, these skills empower  you to navigate adulthood with confidence. Next, we'll jump into job skills and career preparation to ensure you're not just maintaining your home, but also taking care of your future.

Chapter 6
Job Skills and Career Preparation

I magine you're on the brink of a new adventure, ready to step into the world of work, where possibilities are endless, and your future feels like a blank canvas waiting to be painted with your ambitions. But before you dive into that exciting world, there's one crucial tool you'll need: a resume—also sometimes called a CV. (CV stands for Curriculum Vitae, which is Latin for "course of life.") Think of a resume as your personal highlight reel, showcasing your skills, achievements, and experience in a way that makes potential employers do a double-take. It's your first impression in the job application process, a chance to stand out in a sea of applicants and say, "Hey, I'm the one you're looking for!"

A resume is more than just a list of what you've done; it's a snapshot of who you are. It summarizes your qualifications and experiences, painting a picture of your journey so far. Employers use it as a quick guide to gauge if you're the right fit for their team. It's like a movie trailer that teases all the best parts, leaving them eager to learn more. Your resume  highlights your relevant skills and achievements, showing potential employers what you bring to the table. It's your ticket to the interview stage, where you can further charm them with your wit and wisdom.

So, what are the key components of a resume? Let's break it down. First, there's your contact information: name, phone number, and email address. Make sure your email is professional—no "kittylover123" here. An email that contains your first and last name and is as short as possible is a good route to go to look professional. Next is education – list your school(s) from high school and beyond, GPA, and any relevant courses you've taken. Next comes work experience, where you showcase your job history, including job titles, companies, responsibilities, and any notable achievements. Finally, list your skills and certifications. Whether it's computer skills, language proficiency, or organization and project management, this section is your chance to shine. The order of all of the pieces after contact information is negotiable - education, job experience, and skill sets. If you think one of these sections outshines the others as far as actual relevance to the job you are applying for, go ahead and move that section to the top of your resume. You want your strongest points and attention grabbers to always come first. That way employers will want to keep reading past the first glance.

Writing a strong resume involves a few tricks of the trade. Start by using action verbs to describe your responsibilities—words like "managed," "coordinated," or "implemented" add a dynamic flair to your experience. Quantifying achievements is another way to make your resume pop. Instead of saying you "helped increase sales," say you "increased sales by 20%." It gives employers a concrete sense of your impact (but make sure these claims are true and will be backed up by any former employers that your new employer may contact). Tailor your resume to the job description, using language that matches the skills and experience they're looking for. Keep the format clean and professional, with consistent fonts and sizes. Your resume should be easy to read, like a well-organized playlist that flows smoothly from one track to the next.

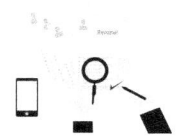

Of course, even the best resume can fall flat if it contains common mistakes. Avoid spelling and grammatical errors like worms on the sidewalk after a rainstorm. They can make your resume look sloppy and unprofessional. Double-check everything, and then check it again. Including irrelevant information is another trap to steer clear of. While your ability to drink 8oz of hot sauce in 12 seconds or paint a Chinese dragon on your fingernails with nail polish might be impressive, it probably won't help you land a job at a tech company. Keep your information relevant to the position. And remember, an unprofessional email address can raise eyebrows for all the wrong reasons. Stick to something simple and straightforward. Finally, aim for the Goldilocks length—not too long, not too short, but just right. A one-page resume is often sufficient, especially if you're just starting your career journey (Larson, 2025).

Wait! I've never worked a job in my life. The closest I've gotten is mowing my lawn for a measly allowance or babysitting my neighbor's kids. How do I make a resume without any job experience??

Don't worry. Even if you've never worked a real job a day in your life, you can still craft an enticing resume. If you have ever done any volunteer service some-where—through a religious organization, school, or other community organization—make sure to showcase that. Also include information about school organizations or clubs you have been a part of, such as chess clubs, peer tutoring programs, school newspapers, or sports teams. All of these sorts of activities teach you valuable skills about time-management, communication, working on a team, problem-solving, or organization. Figure out what you have been a part of that has taught you valuable skills that can transfer to the workplace, and showcase those things. List out for your employer what specific skills your community or school involvement has helped you develop. Again, organize your resume so that your strongest points show up first! If you have not been involved in any community or school programs, think about finding one to get involved in. Having that kind of experience will help employers be more likely to trust you. In the meantime, you can still head-up your resume with any skills that you have that could be relevant to the job and share your education track record. If your resume isn't good enough yet to get the job that you really want, figure out where you can volunteer or work to get experience and gain more skills that will catch the eye of the employers you want to have in the future, and start there!

Take It Back Now: Resume Writing Checklist

Here's a handy checklist to keep your resume on point:

- Include clear contact information with a professional email address.

- List your education, work or volunteer experience, and skills.

- Use action verbs and quantify achievements.

- Tailor your resume to the job description.

- Proofread for spelling and grammatical errors.

- Keep the format clean and professional.

Crafting an impressive resume is like creating a masterpiece that reflects your unique talents and aspirations. It's your chance to make a memorable impression and open doors to exciting career opportunities. So take a deep breath, polish up that resume, and get ready to wow potential employers with your skills and personality. Scan the QR code to check out a sample resume for inspiration:

 Some jobs will also ask for a cover letter with your resume. This gives you the chance to share a little bit of your personality, not just your accomplishments. Format it like a business letter and address it to the hiring manager by name if you can (use Mr. or Ms. So-and-So). If you don't know the hiring manager's name, start with "Dear Hiring Manager." You will use this letter to express why you are interested in this position, what you appreciate about the company, and why you think you are a good fit for both the position and the

company. Briefly highlight your most relevant skills or experience from your resume and give a few more details about how you see those skills or experiences helping you in the new position. Communicate some of your goals or aspirations and how you see the company being a part of you reaching those goals. Even though you are writing in formal, professional language, make sure to let your personality shine through. You can even use a little humor if it seems appropriate. Your personality can grab a potential employer's attention as much as your skill sets can. Keep the cover letter to one page at the most - no more than a few paragraphs - and use clear, precise language. (No endless monologuing about past villainous conquests here.) Close by thanking them for their time and for considering you for the position.

If the employer did not request a cover letter specifically, you might still be able to catch their attention by making a mini-cover-letter out of the email you attach your resume to or in your elevator spiel introduction when you hand them your resume in person. A cover letter is your chance to express in plain language why your skills, education, and personality all fit well with the vision, job requirements, and culture of the company you are applying to.

Job Hunting Strategies for Teens and Young Adults

Venturing into the world of job hunting can feel a bit like navigating a new video game level—exciting, a tad intimidating, but oh-so-rewarding when you get the hang of it. There's a plethora of job opportunities that cater to teens and young adults, each offering a unique experience and the chance to learn new skills. Part-time jobs are a solid starting point, often found in retail or food service, where you can earn some cash and get a taste of responsibility. If you're looking to dive deeper into a specific field, internships and apprenticeships provide hands-on experience, allowing you to learn directly from professionals. Freelance and gig work is gaining popularity, giving you the flexibility to work on projects that align with your interests—think graphic design, writing, or even pet-sitting. Don't overlook volunteer positions either; while they might not pay in cash, they offer invaluable experience and the chance to give back to your community (*Top Ten Job Search Tips for Teens | CareerForce*, 2024).

With your sights set on finding the perfect job, creating a job search plan is your next mission. Start by setting clear goals for what you want to achieve. Are you looking to save for a new bike, gain experience in a particular field, or simply stay busy during the summer? Identifying your objectives helps you focus your search. Next, pinpoint the industries and companies that align with your interests and goals. Research their values, culture,  and the types of roles they offer. Once you've got a list, allocate time each day or week for job search activities. Dedicate time to browsing job boards, sending applications, and reaching out to potential employers. Whenever you can, go in person to introduce yourself to managers with a strong handshake and ask if they are currently hiring. Keep a record of your applications and follow-ups in a journal or spreadsheet. It's like your job search diary, helping you track progress and ensuring no opportunity slips through the cracks. Scan the QR code for a sample tracking spreadsheet:

 Now, let's talk resources. The digital age offers a smorgasbord of tools to help you find job opportunities. Online job boards like Indeed and LinkedIn are treasure troves of openings, allowing you to filter roles by location, industry, and experience level. On top of that, there's networking your own connections. Networking might sound daunting, but it's about connecting with family, friends, or even your neighbor who seems to know everyone. They can offer leads or introductions to potential employers. School career centers and job fairs are gold mines for teens or young adults looking to enter the workforce. They offer guidance, resources, and sometimes even direct connections to employers. Don't underestimate the power of social media either. Platforms like Twitter or Facebook can be excellent for discovering job openings and connecting with industry professionals. And a good old-fashioned Google search can be a good starting point if you're not sure where else to start.

Once you've found some jobs that interest you, crafting a compelling and complete job application is where you get to shine. Start with that personalized cover letter for each job application. It's your chance to introduce yourself and explain why you're the perfect fit for the role. Design your resume to highlight relevant experiences and skills that align with the job description. If you've volunteered at a local animal shelter and you're applying for a pet store position, make that connection clear. When following application instructions, attention to detail can set you apart. If they ask for a specific document format or a particular subject line in the email, make sure to follow those guidelines. Lastly, prepare references and recommendation letters in advance in case the employer requests to see them. Reach out to teachers, mentors, or previous employers who can vouch for your skills, character, and work ethic. Having these ready shows you're proactive and prepared, qualities that employers value.

With these strategies in your toolkit, you're well-equipped to tackle the job hunt with confidence and determination. It's about exploring opportunities, creating a plan, utilizing resources, and crafting applications and resumes that highlight your strengths. So take a deep breath, put on your game face, and get ready to step into the world of work.

Acing the Job Interview

So, you've snagged an interview—congrats! The next step is to prepare like you're getting ready for a big game. Researching the company and the role is your first line of attack. It's like doing your homework on your opponent, so you know their strengths and weaknesses. Dive into their website, check out their social media, and see what they're all about. What are their values? What's their mission? Understanding these can give you a leg up and help you tailor your responses to show you're the perfect fit. Practicing common interview questions is another must. Rope in a friend or a mirror and rehearse until you're not just answering questions, but telling your story. And when it comes to attire, aim for professional but comfortable. Think of your outfit as your armor—something that boosts your confidence while fitting the company's vibe. Lastly, prepare a list of questions to ask your interviewer. This shows you're not just interested in the job, but in the company itself. It's like saying, "Hey, I'm interviewing you too!"

When the big day arrives, you'll likely face some classic interview questions. "Tell me about yourself" might sound simple, but it's your chance to make an impression. Keep it concise—highlight your background, interests, and what led you to this opportunity. For "Why do you want to work here?" focus on what excites you about the role or the company. Maybe it's their innovative approach or their commitment to sustainability. "What are your strengths and weaknesses?" can be tricky. Pick strengths that align with the job and weaknesses that show self-awareness and a desire to improve. For "Describe a challenging situation and how you handled it," think of a time you turned a problem into a learning experience. It's all about showing resilience and problem-solving skills. The key is to answer these questions with honesty and confidence, weaving in your personality and experiences (Doyle, 2024).

Now, let's talk about what you say without words—your body language and communication skills. They speak volumes, often louder than your actual words. Start with eye contact. It shows confidence and engagement, but don't turn it into a staring contest. A firm handshake is your opening act; make it confident but not bone-crushing. When you sit, do so with purpose. Sit up straight, lean slightly forward, and show you're attentive and interested. Avoid those pesky nervous habits like fidgeting or crossing your arms. They can make you seem anxious or closed off. Instead, use your hands naturally to emphasize points, and remember to smile. A genuine smile can break the ice and make the conversation more relaxed for you and your interviewer.

After the interview winds down, your job isn't quite done. Following up is your chance to leave a lasting impression. Start by sending a thank-you email. It's a small gesture, but it goes a long way in showing gratitude and reiterating your interest in the role. In the email, mention something specific from the interview that resonated with you. After you've done that, take some time to personally reflect on your interview performance—what went well and what could you improve? It's not about beating yourself up, but about learning and growing. If the interviewer mentioned contacting your references, give the references a heads-up so they're prepared. And then comes patience. Sometimes responses take a while, but don't let that discourage you. A polite follow-up after a week or two is perfectly fine. It shows persistence and genuine interest without being pushy.

In the end, interviews are as much about finding the right fit for you as they are for the company. So pay attention to whether you liked the people you met during your interview and to what stood out to you about the work environment and general culture of the company from your conversations and observations. If anything stood out as a red flag to you, don't ignore it. There are enough job opportunities out there that you don't need to say 'yes' to a bad fit. Unless you're in desperate need of cash that you can't get by doing some delivery driving on your own, hold out for a job with a good work culture and an employer that will really help you grow and reach your goals. The interview process is your opportunity to showcase your skills and personality and see how they fit into the overall scope of the company, as well as your chance to scope out the vibe of the company and what it would be like to work there. With the right preparation, confidence, and follow-up, you're well on your way to acing the interview and landing that dream job.

Workplace Etiquette and Professionalism

Stepping into the workplace is a bit like entering a new world. Each company has its own unique culture, filled with unspoken rules and expectations. It's like joining a new club where everyone else already knows the secret handshake. Observing and following company norms is your first step in connecting and making a good impression. Pay attention to how your colleagues interact and dress. Dress codes can vary from casual to business formal, so understanding what's expected helps you fit in without feeling out of place. It's also helpful to clarify with your hiring manager what the dress expectation is before the first day of work if that hasn't been addressed yet. Behavior expectations are just as important. Engaging in team activities and meetings shows you're a team player, eager to contribute and learn. It's about finding your rhythm within the group and respecting the traditions that make the workplace tick.

 Professional communication is at the heart of any successful workplace experience. It's not just about what you say, but how you say it. Using formal language in emails and meetings sets the tone for respect and professionalism. Think of it as speaking the workplace language that everyone understands. When answering phones or taking messages, clarity and courtesy go a long way. Imagine you're the friendly voice of the company, making sure messages are delivered accurately and promptly. Addressing colleagues and supervisors respectfully is a must. It's like a verbal high five, showing you value their role and expertise. Listening actively is just as crucial. Listen to understand, not just to respond. Providing constructive feedback shows you're engaged and invested in the team's success, creating an open and collaborative environment.

Managing your time and being punctual are vital skills in the workplace. Arriving on time and meeting deadlines are non-negotiables. They demonstrate reliability and respect for others' time. Prioritizing tasks and managing your workload is like playing a strategic game, ensuring you focus on what's most important without getting overwhelmed. Calendars and task management tools are your allies in this quest. They help keep your schedule organized and deadlines in check. Minimizing distractions during work hours allows you to stay focused and productive. Consider it a challenge to keep your mind on the task at hand, avoiding the temptation of social media or other diversions.

Handling workplace challenges is where your resilience shines. Conflicts with colleagues can arise, but it's how you manage them that sets you apart. Open communication and a willingness to find common ground can turn potential conflicts into opportunities for growth. If you're unsure about something, ask for help or clarification. It's not a sign of weakness, but a commitment to doing the job right. Constructive criticism is another area where grace under pressure is essential. It's not personal; it's a chance to learn and improve. Staying motivated and maintaining a positive attitude will keep you moving forward, even when things get tough. A smile and a can-do spirit can make all the difference, turning challenges into stepping stones. As in all of life, there will be many things in your workplace that you cannot control, but two things you can always choose to control are your attitude and reactions (Reyell, 2024).

In the grand tapestry of life, learning to navigate workplace dynamics is a skill that will serve you well beyond the office walls. It's about growing, adapting, and building con-nections that can last a lifetime. As we close
this chapter, remember that every experience, whether challenging or rewarding, is a chance to learn and grow. In the next chapter, we'll explore the art of communication, a skill that will open doors and deepen relationships, both in and out of the workplace.

Chapter 7

Communication Skills

Active Listening

You're at a concert, the music's pumping, and you're trying to tell your friend something super important. But all they hear is the bass thumping and a couple words. Frustrating, right? Well, sometimes, conversations can feel  just like that even when there's no music blaring—a blur of noise with little understanding. That's where active listening comes into play. It's like turning down the volume on distractions and tuning in to what really matters, allowing you to understand and connect with others in a meaningful way.

Active listening is more than just hearing words; it's about engaging with the speaker fully. It's like being a detective, piecing together clues to uncover the true message. When you actively listen, you're not just waiting for your turn to talk. Instead, you're giving your full attention to the speaker, showing them that their words matter. The benefits are immense. Stronger relationships, better understanding, and smoother conflict resolutions are just the tip of the iceberg. It's like giving your conversations a superpower boost.

The key components of active listening are simple yet powerful. Start by paying full attention to the speaker. Turn off notifications, mentally and physically, so you can focus entirely on the person in front of you. Avoid interruptions like they're your great aunt's stale Christmas fruitcake. It might be tempting to jump in with your thoughts, but holding back allows the speaker to feel heard. Reflecting back and paraphrasing what was said is another crucial element. It's like echoing back the message to ensure you've got it right. And, of course, showing empathy and understanding seals the deal. It's about stepping into the speaker's shoes and seeing the world from their perspective.

Practicing active listening might seem daunting, but with a little effort, it becomes second nature. Role-playing scenarios are a great way to hone these skills. Pretend to be a detective interviewing a witness, focusing on gathering details without interruptions. Listening games and activities can also be fun and educational. Try listening to a podcast or song, then discuss the main points with a friend. It's like training your ears and mind to work in harmony.

Of course, obstacles to active listening are as common as warts on a toad. Distractions and multitasking are major culprits, pulling your focus in a million directions. Combat this by minimizing interruptions, whether it's silencing your phone or finding a quiet space. Preconceived notions and biases can also cloud your ability to listen. It's like wearing tinted glasses that distort the true message. Challenge your assumptions by staying open-minded and curious. When someone expresses an opinion you disagree with, ask more questions to try and understand them more fully instead of rebutting with your opinion. Emotional reactions can hijack your attention, making it hard to focus on the speaker. Acknowledge your feelings but set them aside temporarily. Finally, lack of interest or motivation can make even the most riveting conversation partner feel dull. Find elements in the conversation that pique your curiosity, and ask thoughtful questions to help your conversation partner dive into those specific elements deeper. Remember that everyone has a unique perspective to offer no matter what the conversation topic is.

Listening isn't a natural skill for most people; it's one that we have to put in time and energy to develop through intentional practice! But putting in the effort to get good at listening is absolutely worth it, and you'll see the payoff in richer relationships and healthier communication with the people in your life. Active listening transforms conversations from mundane exchanges into meaningful connections. It's not just about hearing words but understanding the person behind them. Whether you're chatting with friends, family, colleagues, or classmates, these skills open doors to deeper relationships and richer experiences. So, embrace the art of listening and discover the power of truly hearing someone out.

Try It Out: Active Listening Challenge

The next time you have a conversation, challenge yourself to implement active listening techniques:

- Look your conversation partner in the eye while they're talking.

- Lean in slightly and directly face your conversation partner to express interest.

- Instead of thinking about what you want to say next, focus on understanding what your communication partner is really saying and trying to empathize with them.

- Mirror back to them what you heard them say to see if you have understood correctly with phrases like, "What I'm hearing you say is that you feel…" or "It sounds like you think…".

- Allow for pauses in the conversation so that your conversation partner can process further what they've been saying.

- Invite your conversation partner to go deeper with phrases like, "Tell me more about that," "How did you feel when that happened?," or "What good things came out of that?"

- Enjoy deeper and more genuine connection in your conversation!

Check out this QR code for some more interac-
tive listening exercises to grow your skills (Teentalk,
2017):

Constructive Communication in Relationships

You've been there before: you're in a conversation where things start to
heat up, and suddenly it feels like you're in a boxing ring. But instead
of throwing jabs, you're tossing words. This is where building healthy
communication habits can save the day. It starts with using "I" statements instead of "You" statements. Imagine saying, "I feel frustrated
and stressed when plans change last minute," rather than, "You always
change plans at the last minute." See the difference? The first invites
understanding, while the second feels like a verbal jab in the ribs.
Expressing feelings and needs clearly is like turning on a light in a dark
room. It helps others see your perspective without guessing. Honesty and transparency are your trusty sidekicks here. They build trust
and ensure everyone's on the same page. And remember, avoiding
blame and criticism keeps the conversation constructive. Blaming is
like pouring gasoline on a flicker, while constructive communication
is more like setting the stage for a warm campfire on a cold night.

Giving and receiving feedback? It's both an art and a science. When
offering feedback to someone else, think of it as a gift—something that
should be wrapped nicely to say "I care about you." Start with positive
feedback, then address areas for improvement, and finally, close on a
positive note again. This is known as the "sandwich" method, where
you cushion the critique between two positives. It's like serving a
burger, with the critique being the patty and the positives as the buns.
It helps the critique go down easier.

Receiving feedback, on the other hand, requires an open mind and a thick skin. Lis-
ten actively, without jumping to defense. Ask
clarifying questions to help you understand
the feedback better. And remember, feedback
is about growth, not criticism. It's a chance
to stretch and improve. So give any feedback you receive some serious
consideration, and thank your critique partner for having the courage
to speak up and share their thoughts honestly. That's not always easy
to do.

Non-verbal communication is the silent orchestra playing in the
background of every conversation. Body language and facial expressions can speak louder than words. A nod says "I'm with you," while
crossed arms can signal defensiveness or insecurity. Tone of voice adds
color to your words, making "I'm fine" sound anything but fine. Eye
contact is the glue that holds a conversation together. It shows engagement and interest. Gestures and postures are the dance moves
of communication. They add flair and emphasis, helping convey the
true meaning behind your words. If you point your feet away from
the person you are talking to, it indicates you are ready to leave the
conversation. Leaning toward someone while they are talking to you
communicates that you are invested in what they are saying. Smiling at
someone communicates openness and an invitation to engage in conversation. Sitting and standing up straight communicates confidence
and intentionality. Slouching communicates insecurity, laziness, or
being closed off. It's like painting a picture with invisible brushstrokes,
creating a full and vivid image.

Handling difficult conversations can feel like walking a tightrope.
But with the right approach, you can keep your balance. Preparation
is key. Think about what you want to say and how to say it. It's

like rehearsing for a play, ensuring your message comes across clearly. Prepare a time and place where you and the person you need to talk through something with will both be able to engage in the conversation well. Often, serious disagreements should not be addressed in the moment they first rear their heads because emotions will get in the way of a healthy conversation. Staying calm and composed is crucial, even if emotions run high. Take deep breaths and maintain a steady demeanor. Finding common ground can be a game-changer. Focus on shared interests or goals to create a foundation for understanding. And sometimes, it's okay to agree to disagree. It's not about winning or losing; it's about maintaining respect and connection. Maintaining healthy connections and open lines of communication with people in your life is better than winning an argument any day. We'll dive into conflict resolution more in a moment, since that's a topic that deserves its own spotlight.

When you combine these skills, you're not just communicating; you're connecting on a deeper level.

Boundaries in Relationships

While you may not need to learn how to build brick walls or set up yard fences, setting boundaries in relationships is an important skill to develop. If you find your interactions with a specific person in your life creating a pattern of negative emotions for you, you may need to communicate and uphold some boundaries with them. That need can arise with members of your own family, in your school environment, at work, or even with neighbors or mere acquaintances. Setting a boundary is recognizing that we can't control what other people say or do, but we can control how we will respond in certain situations. For example, let's say your aunt brings up politics every time she starts talking to you and makes very derogatory remarks toward you or your political stance in every conversation you have. You can ask her to not bring up politics around you, but that is not a boundary. That's a request, and she can choose whether to honor your request or not.

Alternatively, you can set a boundary by saying something like this, "Aunt Bertha, I am not comfortable discussing politics with you because I don't feel like I am able to have a different opinion when I am around you, and  when you bring up that subject from now on, I will have to leave the conversation so that we can have a healthier relationship." Then when she does bring up politics again next time she sees you, you politely excuse yourself from the conversation to keep the boundary you have communicated. Boundaries are a response that you can control to situations that arise.

Let's look at one more example of boundary-setting since this is such an important skill to learn. Let's say that your best friend thinks it's okay to use drugs recreationally sometimes, and he brings drugs with him when he comes to hang out with you often—even though he knows you don't feel comfortable with using drugs illegally for fun. You've asked him several times now not to use drugs around you, and you've told him many times that you don't want to try them. But he keeps asking you to join him anyway. You don't want to lose him as a friend, but it's time to set a boundary. Your boundary conversation could sound something like this: "Cody, I care about you and about our friendship, but I am not okay with you using drugs around me and trying to get me to do drugs with you. From now on, if you show up to hang out with me and you are under the influence of drugs, I won't be able to stay and hang out. And if you invite me to use drugs with you at any point when we're together, I will have to leave." In order for this to be a legitimate boundary, the next step is to follow through consistently on the expectation you have set without making exceptions. The next time your friend shows up high, tell him you guys can try for a hang-out again on another day when he's sober and then leave the situation.

It may feel like setting boundaries puts your relationships in danger, but the opposite is actually true. If you can learn how to set and communicate healthy boundaries in your relationships, you will be better equipped to build lasting, worthwhile relationships in every area of your life. What does put your relationships in danger is resentment and bitterness that start building up inside you when you don't set healthy boundaries and instead begin to feel manipulated, misused, or attacked by people in your life who can't honor requests that you've made of them. As long as you communicate your boundaries in a way that is respectful and honest, and maintain those boundaries with the same respect, boundaries will help you set your relationships on a trajectory toward greater health and happiness over time!

Conflict Resolution Strategies

Conflict—it's as unavoidable as the sun rising in the east. At its core, conflict is a clash of interests, needs, or values. It can be as minor as a disagreement over movie choices or as significant as differing opinions on major life decisions. The causes of conflict are as varied as a box of chocolates—unvoiced expectations, miscommunication, and unmet needs are just a few examples. When conflicts go unresolved, they can fester and grow, leading to greater tension and seriously damaged relationships. It's like letting dirty dishes pile up in the sink; sooner or later, you'll have a major mess on your hands (Pollack, 2024).

Dealing with conflict isn't about avoiding it because, let's face it, that's like trying to dodge raindrops in a storm. Instead, it's about choosing how you respond. Some people are naturally avoiders, side-stepping conflict like it's a puddle on the sidewalk. While this might keep things calm temporarily, it doesn't solve the underlying issue and tends to lead to even bigger problems over time. Others might accommodate, putting the other person's needs ahead of their own. It's a noble gesture but can lead to resentment when used repeatedly. Then there's competing, where one person pushes to "win" the argument, leaving the other feeling completely unheard and potentially causing long-term damage to the relationship. Compromising finds a middle ground, where both parties give a little to reach an agreement. Collaborating, on the other hand, aims for a win-win solution, where everyone's needs are met. It's like finding the perfect playlist that makes everyone happy.

Resolving conflicts constructively is a bit like assembling a puzzle. Start by identifying the root cause of the conflict. This might take some digging, like figuring out why your phone isn't charging. Often, the thing the argument is about isn't the same as the thing that the conflict is about. This can get really deep really fast, but it's super important to be aware of. For example, your friend's blow-up about you showing up late to give her a ride may initially seem like a ridiculous overreaction. But what if you learned that she grew up in a home where she could never rely on her parents to come through and do what they promised they would do, leaving her feeling like she couldn't trust other people and always needed to look out for herself. So now, even small inconsistencies in keeping your word (like showing up late) get interpreted by her as "I don't care about you or your needs, so don't rely on me"

– the message she got from her parents growing up. In a situation like this, both parties have work to do to handle the conflict healthily. Open and honest communication is key. It might feel as awkward as wearing socks with sandals, but it's vital. Listen to understand, not just to reply. Seek to understand the other person's perspective, and ask questions about thoughts, emotions, and background to help you both get at the root of what is going on. It's like trying on someone else's glasses; the world looks different through their lens. Sometimes, this process takes time and reflection, and you may need to come back to the conversation once you have both had some time to reflect on why you responded the way you did in that situation. Especially if the level of emotional response in the situation seemed too big for the circumstance, it's time for both parties to do some reflection and digging to find out what history was being brought into that moment. Once you both see the bigger picture, work together to find mutually acceptable solutions. This might involve a little give-and-take, but the goal is to find a resolution that satisfies everyone involved and acknowledges both people's experiences as "real."

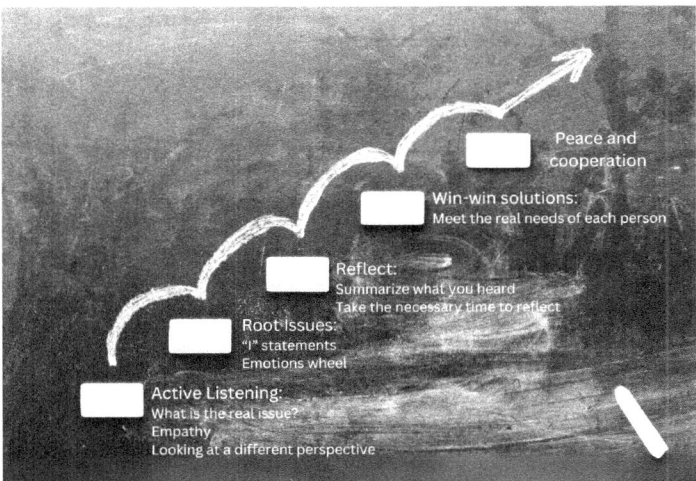

If you find yourself in a repeating conflict that feels like it's spiraling into a tornado, mediation and negotiation skills come in handy. As previously mentioned, active listening and empathy are your best friends here. They help you understand the emotions behind the words, turning potential arguments into discussions. It can also be helpful to set ground rules for discussions before they come up to ensure they stay productive. For example, if you find yourself frequently arguing with your parents about how you spend your time even though you are an adult not living in their home anymore, you might need to initiate a conversation to set some new ground rules and make clear what each other's expectations are. (Pro tip: don't try to set the ground rules in the middle of an argument; take some time and space, and come back to the conversation when you're calm and have had time to do some honest evaluation of the part you play in the problem.) Setting ground rules in the instance of the above example with your parents might mean a conversation where you sit down with your parents and communicate something along these lines:

"I'm super grateful for everything you guys did for me growing up and for all the work you put into helping me become the best person I can be, but I need some time and space to shape my life on my own and to practice making my own decisions as an adult now. I still want you to be a part of my life, but I feel like I can't share my life with you without it turning into a conflict. Can we agree that when I share things about my life that you disagree with, you can tell me you disagree without trying to make me change my mind or make me feel guilty? I still need you in my corner as my parents, but I also need to figure some things out on my own right now. Can we work on making our relationship a safe place for me to communicate my experiences as I figure out how to be an adult?"

Do you see how communicating your needs and setting ground rules in this way could be a game changer? Now I want to point out some techniques that I used in crafting this conversation starter that can be used in any conversation to create an atmosphere for healthier communication:

1. I started with calling to mind our common ground and common goals – We belong to the same family; we both have my best interest in mind and want me to become the best adult I can be.

2. I used what is called a "soft start"; I purposely launched with gratitude and made sure not to start with any kind of accusations or blame throwing, which would immediately put the other party on the defensive and make it hard for them to actually hear what I want to say.

3. I used "I" statements instead of "You" statements - "when such and such happens, I feel…", "right now, I need…", or "I still want…". Using "I" statements creates an atmosphere where you are able to be honest about your experience without assuming what the other party's motivations or intentions are. Instead of saying, "You always judge me when I share about my life," say, "I feel judged when I try to tell you about my life." This leaves space for the other party to communicate what is actually happening on their end, which may be completely different than what you're experiencing on your end. This is very important if any real understanding or reconciliation is ever going to take place – because you know what they say about assuming? (If not, Google it.)

Using these three techniques – finding common ground, the "soft start," and using "I" statements – are the secret weapons of conflict resolution. If both parties agree to use these techniques when there's a conflict, it's like having a referee in a game—everyone knows the rules, and things stay fair. But even if only you use these techniques, it can still make your disagreements into way more effective conversations. Even so, sometimes it might be necessary to seek outside help, like a mediator or counselor, to facilitate the discussion. And that is totally okay. Remember, asking for help isn't a sign of weakness; it's another strategy for success.

Navigating conflicts can feel like walking through a maze, but with the right approach, you can find your way through. Understanding the nature of conflict, choosing effective resolution styles, and applying constructive strategies are all part of the process. Whether it's a minor disagreement or a major dispute, these skills empower you to handle conflicts with greater confidence and clarity.

Public Speaking Tips and Tricks

Ah, public speaking—the thought alone might send shivers down your spine. Whether it's presenting in front of a classroom, speaking at a club meeting, or even just answering a question in a large group, the mere idea can make your palms sweaty and your heart race. This fear, known as  public speaking anxiety, is something many people grapple with. It's that feeling of being in the spotlight, with everyone's eyes on you, waiting for every word that will come out of your mouth. But here's the good news: you can tame this beast. Start by understanding that nervousness is natural; it's your body's way of gearing up for action. Embrace it as a sign that you care. Techniques like deep breathing help calm those jittery nerves. Visualize success—imagine yourself speaking confidently and engagingly. Positive self-talk is another powerful tool. Remind yourself that you've got this, and soon enough, your mind will believe it too. Practicing relaxation techniques, like mindfulness exercises or simple body stretches, also helps focus your mind, bringing a sense of calm before taking the stage.

Now, let's talk preparation. Preparing a speech or presentation is like building a house; it requires a solid foundation. Begin by researching your topic thoroughly. The better you know your material, the more confident you'll feel. Organize your content logically, creating a roadmap that guides your audience through your speech. Use clear notes, keeping them concise but informative, like a trusty guidebook. Practice your speech multiple times in front of a mirror or with a friend. This helps you get comfortable with the flow and identify areas that need tweaking. Remember, practice doesn't make perfect, but it does make progress.

Delivering a speech effectively is an art in itself. Maintain eye contact with your audience to create a connection, letting your eyes move naturally around the room to different people to keep the whole room engaged. (If that feels terrifying, you can start by keeping your gaze just above their heads; especially in a large room, this gives the illusion of eye contact to your audience.) That way, it's like having a conversation, rather than reciting a script. Use gestures and body language to emphasize your points, adding a dynamic element to your delivery. Vary your tone and pace for emphasis, keeping your audience engaged. Storytelling or asking questions can also draw the audience in, making your speech more relatable and memorable. And smile! Smiling not only makes your audience feel more comfortable, it can also actually reduce your anxiety.

 Handling questions and feedback can feel like navigating a minefield, but it's an opportunity to shine. Prepare for common questions by considering possible queries and crafting thoughtful responses. When a question arises, listen carefully to ensure you understand it fully. Respond thoughtfully, addressing the question directly and respectfully. It's okay if you don't know the answer—acknowledging this and offering to find out later shows integrity. For difficult or unexpected questions, stay calm and composed. It's like a dance; sometimes, you lead, and sometimes, you follow. Approach each question with an open mind, and remember that every interaction is a chance to learn and grow (*Fear of Public Speaking: How Can I Overcome It?*, n.d.).

As we wrap up this chapter on communication skills, remember that public speaking is a journey of discovery. Each opportunity to speak is a chance to learn, grow, and connect with others. Embrace the challenge, knowing that every stumble is a step toward becoming a more confident and effective communicator.

In the next chapter, we'll dive into developing emotional intelligence, a key component of understanding yourself and others. With communication skills in your toolkit, you're ready to explore the world of emotions and empathy.

Chapter 8

Developing Emotional Intelligence

E ver had one of those days where your emotions seem to be playing a game of musical chairs? One moment you're ecstatic, the next, you're feeling all sorts of grumpy for no apparent reason. It's like your feelings decided to throw a surprise party and forgot to invite your brain. Welcome to the world of emotions, where understanding and managing them is like being the conductor of a very lively orchestra. The key is learning how to identify and name each instrument—or emotion—in your band.

Start by building your emotional vocabulary. Think of it as expanding your personal dictionary of feelings. Words like happy, sad, anxious, and excited are just the tip of the iceberg. Expanding your emotional vocabulary is the first step to expanding your emotional awareness. For example, experiencing disappointment is different than experiencing regret, but if you refer to them both as 'being sad,' you miss out on an opportunity to be known well by those near to you and to effectively respond to your emotions. Experiencing disappointment could be a wake-up call that you need to clarify your expectations with someone and make sure you are both on the same page. Regret might tell you that you need to ask someone for forgiveness, or do something to correct a mistake you made. But if you just call both of those emotions sadness, you may end up thinking that what you need to do is just sit and cry for a little while. (There is nothing wrong with crying. Sometimes that is the best response, or an important piece of responding, to an emotion. But do you see how giving emotions a more precise name opens up the door for more defined action steps in response?) Journaling can be a huge help here, letting you track your emotions and spot patterns over time. It's like keeping a diary of your inner world, revealing how different situations make you feel. And for a fun twist, try using an emotion wheel. These colorful charts help you pinpoint exactly what you're feeling, transforming vague emotions into specific, nameable states.

Wheel of Emotions

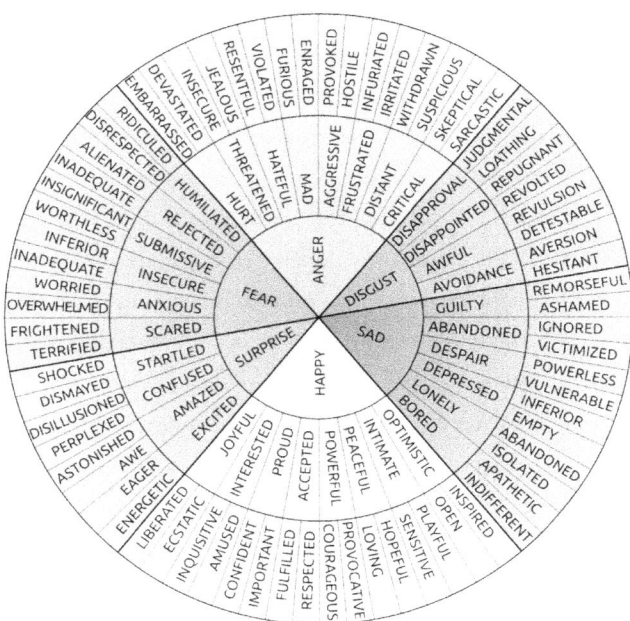

Understanding what causes your emotions is like solving a mystery. Sometimes you're alerted by those butterflies in your stomach before a big exam or the way your heart races when you're about to speak in front of the class. These physical sensations are often your body's way of signaling an emotional response. Situational triggers, like a family argument or an encounter with someone you don't get along with, can also stir up strong feelings. And let's not forget about those tricky thought patterns and beliefs that can sneak up on you because of how you were raised, shaping how you perceive and react to the world.

When emotions run high, having strategies to manage them can make a world of difference. Deep breathing exercises are like a reset button for your nervous system, helping calm the storm inside. Breathe in through your nose and out through your mouth to help activate your parasympathetic nervous system, which puts your body in a state of rest instead of stress. Progressive muscle relaxation works wonders, too, by easing tension from head to toe. Close your eyes while you breathe deeply, and notice where your muscles feel tense. With each exhale, focus on intentionally relaxing one muscle at a time. Picture it as a mini-vacation for your muscles, where each muscle gets to step onto the beach one at a time. Grounding techniques, like focusing on your senses, can anchor you in the present moment when anxiety tries to whisk you away. One good grounding technique is the 5,4,3,2,1 technique. Start by focusing on what you can see with your eyes and notice 5 details in the environment around you. Then turn your attention to what you feel with your body and identify 4 things you feel - like the warmth of the sun or the socks on your feet. Next, notice 3 things that you can hear wherever you are. After that, find 2 things that you smell right now. Finally, focus on 1 thing you can taste. If you're anxious and find yourself stuck in your head, this sort of grounding technique helps you get back in touch with your body and reality in the present moment. And lastly, never underestimate the power of a stress ball or fidget toy—they're a friendly outlet for nervous energy.

Building emotional resilience is akin to training for a marathon. It takes practice, but the rewards are worth it. Cognitive reframing is a powerful tool, allowing you to shift negative thought patterns into more positive perspectives. To practice cognitive reframing, notice when you are thinking about a situation or person negatively. Then ask yourself, "Is there another way I could look at this situation?" Consider some more positive or even more realistic alternatives. For example, if someone cuts me off on the highway, I might find myself thinking, "Wow, what a jerk! You just think the whole road belongs to you and I don't matter at all, don't you?!"

When I catch myself creating a negative narrative for the situation, I can pause and ask myself what other interpretations there might be for what just happened instead of assuming that the person is just reckless and selfish. Maybe he's driving his pregnant wife to the hospital to give birth. Maybe his Great Aunt Bertha is dying alone in the nursing home, and he's on his way to be with her. Maybe his boss told him if he's  late for work one more time he'll be fired. Maybe he just forgot to check his blind spot before he started merging into my lane. All of these possibilities are actually just as likely as the negative narrative I came up with initially, and if I choose to settle on one of these new, more positive narratives instead of the negative narrative, my mood and my day are instantly improved. You can use this technique with people you know well too, not just strangers. Instead of assuming your friend hates you because she ignored your calls for three days, give her the benefit of the doubt and wonder whether she broke her phone and hasn't gotten a new one or whether she's super depressed right now and finding it hard to communicate that to other people. The more often you catch your negative stories and assumptions and reframe them into more positive possibilities, the better your brain will get at doing it. And over time, your brain might actually automatically go to writing a positive story for the situation instead of a negative one. And that leads to way more good days than bad days!

A few more simple tips: practicing gratitude can help boost your resilience, helping you see the silver linings even on cloudy days. Consider starting or ending your day by thinking about 5 things you are grateful for every day. Setting realistic goals and expectations keeps you grounded, providing a sense of direction and purpose. And engaging in regular physical activity gives your emotions a healthy outlet, releasing endorphins that elevate your mood and strengthen your resilience.

Put It Into Practice: Emotion Journaling Prompt

Grab your journal and take a few minutes each day to jot down feelings that you experienced throughout the day. Use an emotion wheel to help identify specific emotions. Reflect on any triggers that caused strong emotions or caused physical sensations you noticed during the day that alerted you that you were experiencing an emotion. Over time, this practice can enhance your emotional intelligence, providing insights into your emotional landscape. You may notice patterns of emotions that come up for you in certain situations or around certain people. If you do notice a pattern, you might take some time to reflect on whether anyone else in your family seems to have some of the same patterns or even a directly opposite pattern. Sometimes, we either mimic or oppose patterns that we've experienced in our family, depending on our relationship with the person who expresses that emotional pattern. This isn't necessarily a bad thing, but recognizing if you are doing that can help you be aware of whether the emotions you are experiencing in a certain situation are actually how *you* feel or just a response you've learned to have because of past experiences.

Recognizing and managing your emotions isn't about avoiding the roller coaster—it's about strapping in and enjoying the ride, with all its ups and downs. By understanding your feelings and building resilience, you empower yourself to navigate life's challenges with confidence and grace.

Building Empathy and Compassion

 Imagine standing in someone else's shoes, feeling their joys and sorrows as if they were your own. That's empathy, the ability to truly understand and connect with others on a deep emotional level. It's like having a secret superpower that strengthens your relationships and helps you relate to those around you. But beware, empathy is often confused with its distant cousin, sympathy. While sympathy involves feeling concern or pity for someone, empathy is all about experiencing someone's emotions from their perspective, like seeing the world through their eyes. Empathy builds bridges and fosters stronger connections, enabling you to listen without judgment and offer genuine support (Chan, 2023).

Practicing active listening is a great way to show empathy, as discussed in Chapter 7. When you listen empathetically, you reflect the speaker's feelings and words, like holding up a mirror to their emotions. Nodding and maintaining eye contact show that you're present and engaged, creating a safe space where they feel heard. Asking open-ended questions invites them to share more, deepening your understanding and strengthening your connection. Open-ended questions are questions that can't be answered with a 'yes' or 'no'. They often start with 'what' or 'how'. For example, a closed question would be: "Was it scary for you the first time you stayed at home alone?" To make this question open-ended and invite a fuller response, ask: "What was it like for you the first time you stayed at home alone? How did you feel?" Don't be afraid of silences in the conversation either. Moments of silence create space for someone to continue processing and thinking, and if you give them space, they may be able to share even more deeply with you than if you forced them to move on to a new thought by asking a follow-up question right away. If you're not sure what emotions someone might be experiencing while they share something with you, sometimes it can help to physically mirror their body's position or their face's expression and see what emotions those postures or expressions create in you. (But don't be awkward or exaggerated about it. If you can't do this naturally in the conversation, just picturing yourself in the body posture or facial expression can sometimes help you get a gauge on what emotions the other person might be experiencing.)

But empathy doesn't stop at understanding others; it's about cultivating compassion too. Volunteering for community service allows you to see the world from different perspectives, broadening your horizons and opening your heart. Performing random acts of kindness, whether it's helping a neighbor or offering a compliment, spreads positivity like ripples in a pond. Practicing self-compassion is equally important. It involves treating yourself with kindness and understanding, especially when things don't go as planned. It's like being your own best friend, offering encouragement instead of criticism.

Empathy-building exercises can help you fine-tune this skill. Role-playing different perspectives allows you to step into someone else's shoes, challenging you to see situations from new angles. Reading stories or watching movies with strong emotional content invites you to explore complex emotions and reflect on your reactions. Participating in empathy workshops or groups provides a space to share experiences and learn from others, fostering a sense of community and mutual understanding.

Test It: Empathy Role-Playing Exercise

Gather a group of friends and try role-playing different scenarios, such as a misunderstanding between classmates or a family disagreement. Take turns being the person to choose the scenario and assign everyone their initial role, then play out the scene multiple times, rotating who plays which role each time. After each role, discuss how it feels to be in that person's shoes before moving on to playing a different role in the same scene. Once everyone has gotten a chance to play all the roles in a scene, a new person gets to create a new scene and assign starting roles. This exercise encourages empathy and helps you see situations from multiple perspectives, enhancing your emotional intelligence. (If your friends aren't the type to want to grow in emotional intelligence with you, present this exercise as a "Whose Line Is It Anyway?" game, and you might have better luck getting them to join you!)

Building empathy and compassion isn't about being perfect. It's about being present, open, and willing to connect with others in meaningful ways. So, next time you face a challenging interaction, take a moment to consider the other person's perspective. It might just change your own.

Navigating Peer Pressure and Bullying

Peer pressure can feel like a giant wave, sweep-
ing you up and carrying you in directions you
never intended to go. It happens because social
dynamics create an environment where fitting in
seems like the most important thing. There are
different types of peer pressure—direct, where
someone explicitly tells you what to do, and in-

direct, where you feel the need to conform because everyone else is
doing it. It can be positive, like when friends encourage you to study
harder, or negative, like when you're urged to try something dangerous or unhealthy. Picture a cafeteria scene: everyone's talking about a
party where there will be some not-so-legal activities taking place, and
suddenly, you're torn between going because you want to fit in and
staying true to your values. It's all about influence and the desire to
belong, which can make standing your ground tricky.

Resisting negative peer pressure is like flexing a muscle—it gets
stronger with practice. Start with assertive communication. It's your
superpower for setting boundaries and expressing your thoughts
clearly without being confrontational. Practice saying "no" confidently, like it's the most natural word in your vocabulary. Maintaining a
strong sense of self and values also acts as a shield, helping you decide
what's right for you. Surround yourself with trusted allies—friends
and adults who support you when you make healthy decisions and
offer good advice (sometimes good advice is not the same as the advice
you want to hear at the moment). Having a backup plan can ease
the pressure, like using a secret code with parents or a trusted mentor to signal when you need an escape route from a sticky situation

(*How to Handle Peer Pressure*, n.d.). You can also communicate clear boundaries to your friends before a situation arises that makes you feel pressured so that they already know what you are and are not willing to do. This can make saying "no" in the moment easier too.

Bullying as you move out of school and into the workplace can show up as a different beast altogether. Recognizing the signs is crucial—unexplained injuries, changes in behavior, and reluctance to engage with peers are red flags. Handling sexual misconduct, harassment, discrimination, or abuse in the workplace is serious, but knowing what to do can empower you to take action if it happens to you or someone else. First, trust your instincts—if something feels wrong or makes you uncomfortable, it's okay to speak up. If directly addressing the issue with the person doesn't work or feels unsafe, start by documenting everything: write down what happened, when, where, and who was involved. Report it to your supervisor or human resources manager (HR), as they're trained to handle these situations. If that feels too intimidating, confide in a trusted coworker or mentor for support, but make sure someone else knows and there is written documentation so that they can vouch for you if more witnesses are needed. For more serious situations or if supervisors are a part of the problem, you can contact external resources like the Equal Employment Opportunity Commission (EEOC) for advice or to file a complaint (EEOC, 2023). If it escalates to a criminal level, call law enforcement or seek help from organizations like the Rape, Abuse & Incest National Network (RAINN) through their hotline at 1-800-656-HOPE or their online chat service (RAINN, 2023). Don't ever put off reporting an issue because there are specific time limits connected with filing different types of reports and complaints. If there is a serious problem, don't hesitate to get help! Remember, you deserve to feel safe and respected at work—don't let anyone tell you otherwise.

Building a positive peer group is like planting a garden. It requires nurturing and attention but results in a supportive network that thrives on trust and mutual respect. Look for friends who lift you up, not drag you down. Healthy friendships are rooted in shared interests and values, creating a space where you can be yourself without fear of judgment. Engage in activities that promote positive interactions, like joining clubs or teams where collaboration and teamwork are key. And remember, avoiding toxic relationships is vital. If someone consistently puts you down or disrespects you, it might be time to reevaluate that friendship.

Building and Maintaining Healthy Relationships

Imagine relationships as a delicate dance, where mutual respect and trust are the rhythm that keeps everything in harmony. In healthy relationships, both parties feel valued and appreciated, like partners who can rely on each other through thick and thin. Effective communication is the key to this dance, ensuring that both sides understand and support each other. When equality and fairness are present, no one feels like they're carrying the weight of the world alone; instead, both partners share the load. Emotional support and understanding act as the safety net, so that you can catch each other when things get tough. It's about being there, not just in the good times, but also when the chips are down (Jivanjee et al., 2016).

But how do you build these strong connections? Start with active listening and open communication. I've brought up these points over and over, but these are like the glue that holds relationships together, allowing each person to feel known and valued. Conflict resolution and problem-solving skills come next, acting as the tools that help navigate the inevitable bumps along the way. Showing appreciation and gratitude regularly is like watering a plant; it helps relationships grow and flourish. Setting and respecting boundaries is crucial too. It ensures that both parties feel comfortable and secure, knowing that their personal space and needs are honored.

Recognizing unhealthy patterns in relationships is like spotting weeds in a garden. These might include manipulation, control, or a lack of respect. Addressing these issues requires honesty and courage. It might involve having difficult conversations or even seeking help from trusted friends or counselors. Sometimes, despite our best efforts, a relationship might not be salvageable. Knowing when to end it is crucial for your well-being. It's okay to step away from relationships that consistently bring negativity or distress into your life.

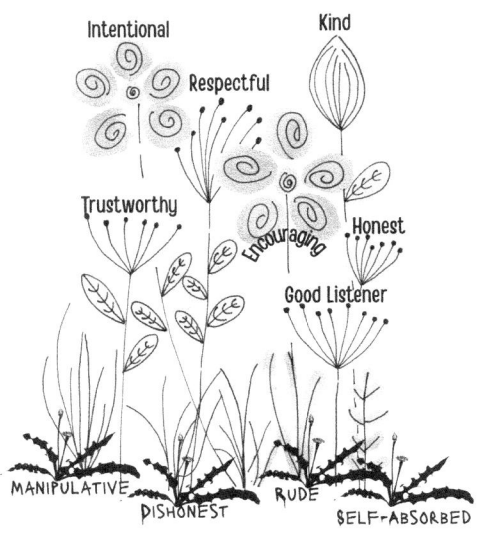

Self-awareness is another cornerstone of healthy relationships. Understanding your own needs and emotions allows you to communicate them clearly to others. Reflecting on your behavior and its impact on those around you helps you grow and improve. It's like looking in a mirror to ensure you're presenting your best self. Practicing self-improvement is an ongoing journey, one that benefits not only you but also the people you care about. Seeking feedback from trusted friends and family can provide valuable insights and help you see things from a fresh perspective. They're the ones who can offer honest reflections, nudging you towards becoming a better version of yourself. Try asking someone who knows you well what it's like to have you as a friend or to live with you—both the good and the bad. Hear them out without getting defensive or coming up with explanations for behaviors they might bring up. Then take some time to reflect on your own about what they shared and whether there are things you can do to improve your relationship skills based on things they shared with you.

In the end, building and maintaining healthy relationships is about creating connections that uplift and support you. It's about surrounding yourself with people who celebrate your successes and stand by you during challenges. It's about being open, honest, and willing to grow, both individually and together. With these principles in mind, you're well on your way to nurturing relationships that enrich your life and bring out the best in you.

Building a Support Network

Have you ever noticed how every successful hero has a sidekick that keeps them on track? Frodo has Sam. Han Solo has Chewy. Sherlock has Watson. The list goes on. Similarly, your success is reinforced by your personal support network. That's the group of people who offer emotional encouragement, practical advice, and assistance when you're in a pinch. They help you navigate life's twists and turns, providing guidance and lending a hand with problem-solving and decision-making. Having a strong support network is like having a personal cheering squad, boosting your overall well-being and helping you face challenges with confidence and resilience.

Identifying potential members of your support network is like assembling your dream team. Start with family members and close relatives—they've known you forever and usually have your best interests at heart. Friends and peers come next; they're the ones who understand the ins and outs of your daily life. Teachers, mentors, and coaches can provide wisdom beyond your years, offering insights and advice from their own experiences. Community groups and organizations are also fantastic resources, connecting you with like-minded individuals. Don't underestimate the power of intergenerational relationships, either. Connecting with people from different age groups can offer fresh perspectives and valuable life lessons, making your network even more robust.

Maintaining and strengthening these relationships requires effort, but the rewards are worth it. Regular communication and check-ins keep the communication lines open, ensuring that everyone feels valued and connected. Showing appreciation and gratitude lets your support network know how much they mean to you. Being reliable and trustworthy builds a foundation of mutual respect, while offering support in return creates an environment of give-and-take. It's like tending a garden: with care and attention, your relationships will flourish, providing support when you need it most.

Expanding your support network is an adventure waiting to happen. Joining clubs and organizations is a great way to meet new people who share your interests. Volunteering for community service not only helps others but also introduces you to individu-als who value giving back. Attending social events and networking opportunities can open doors to new friendships and connections. Don't be afraid to reach out and ask someone to have coffee or go for a walk one-on-one to get to know them better. And in today's digital age, social media and online communities offer endless possibilities for expanding your network. (Practice safety in online relationships and don't share personal identifying information unless you've gotten to know someone in person in a safe public space first, please!) Building your support network is like casting a wide net, inviting positivity and support into your life.

Do It: Name Your Support Network

Pull out a journal and list out who your support network is right now. Does it include both peers and mentor figures? If not, who do you need to start spending time with to have a more well-rounded support network? What steps can you take to enhance the connections you do have and bring more intentionality and open communication into your relationships?

In the grand scheme of things, your support network plays a pivotal role in your journey toward emotional intelligence and personal growth. As you build and nurture these connections, you'll find your-self better equipped to face life's challenges with a sense of confidence and assurance. Now, as we wrap up this chapter, take a moment to appreciate the power of your support network and the strength it brings to your life. With this foundation in place, you're ready to explore the next chapter, where we'll delve into the world of internet safety and digital literacy, ensuring that your virtual interactions are just as rewarding and secure as your real-world connections.

Make a Difference with Your Review

Unlock the Power of Generosity

"The best way to predict your future is to create it." – Abraham Lincoln

Hey, you! Yes, you! Let's take a moment to talk about something pretty cool: helping others. You know that warm, fuzzy feeling you get when you do something kind, like sharing your last slice of pizza or helping someone understand their homework? Well, guess what—leaving a review for *Adulting Like a Boss* is just like that!

Imagine this: someone, just like you, is curious about figuring out this whole adulting thing but doesn't know where to start. They're scrolling through a bunch of books, wondering which one might actually help (and not be boring). That's where *you* come in.

I wrote *Adulting Like a Boss* to make adulting feel less like climbing a mountain and more like shredding on a skateboard (while wearing a helmet, of course). But the only way more people can find it is through honest reviews from amazing readers like you.

Here's the deal:

Your review doesn't have to be fancy. Just a few words about what you liked, maybe your favorite tip, or how it helped you. It takes less than a minute, costs absolutely nothing, and could totally change someone's journey from "What is this adulting madness?" to "I got this!"

Your review could:

- Help one more young adult tackle their first apartment.

- Inspire one more person to crush their budgeting fears.

- Show someone they're not alone in figuring this stuff out.

- Make one more dream feel totally doable.

Ready to be awesome? Just scan the QR code to leave your review!

 If you've ever wondered if small actions can make a big difference, this is proof they can. Thanks for helping others—and for being a total boss!

High-five!

![QR code]

SCAN ME

Chapter 9

Internet Safety and Digital Literacy

Protecting Personal Information

I magine for a moment that the internet is like a bustling city. It's filled with amazing sights, endless entertainment, and even a few shady alleyways you should probably avoid. Just like in any city, knowing how to protect yourself is key to having a great experience. Online, your personal information is like your passport—it's precious, and you'd better not hand it over to just anyone. So let's dive into how to keep that digital passport safe and sound.

Understanding what qualifies as personal information is the first step to keeping it secure. It includes obvious details like your full name, address, and phone number. These are the pieces of info that, if they were puzzle pieces, would almost complete the picture of who you are.

Then there's the more sensitive stuff: your Social Security number, bank account details, passwords, and security questions. These are like the access codes to your digital kingdom, and you want to keep them under lock and key. Even photos and videos can be personal information, especially if they reveal things you'd rather keep private. It might not seem like a big deal if someone random on the internet gets access to your phone number. What are they gonna do? Spam call you until you block their number? But what happens is that those little "insignificant" bits of information get sold on the black market. As different sources get access to different small pieces of your information, the buyers of that information are able to piece together a clearer and clearer picture of who you are, one small detail at a time.

Eventually, this can lead to real-ly serious problems like credit fraud and identity theft. Get in the habit of not sharing your personal information with anyone you don't know unless you have verified that they are a trusted  company or individual. A quick Google search for reviews on the company or a check for their Better Business Bureau rating can help you figure out whether a company or individual offering you services is probably legit or not.

Creating strong passwords is like building a fortress around your personal information. They need to be long, complex, and unique, much like a secret handshake only you know. A good password should include a mix of letters, numbers, and symbols—think of it as a digital smoothie with lots of ingredients. Avoid using common words or phrases that someone could easily guess, like "password123." Change your passwords regularly to keep them fresh, like replacing old socks with new ones. And if remembering all those complex passwords feels like juggling greasy spaghetti noodles, consider using a password manager. These handy tools store your passwords securely and can even generate strong ones for you (*Internet Safety: Creating Strong Passwords*, n.d.). A good old fashioned written list can work too. Just keep it in a safe place.

Recognizing phishing and scams is another crucial skill in the digital age. They can be wild and obvious or well-disguised and tricky. Let's say you receive an email from a prince in eastern Europe offering you a fortune because he found out you are actually long-lost cousins. He's ready to transfer that fortune to you right now if you just send your bank details. Sounds fishy, right? But what if you get a call about the warranty on your car expiring, and they say you need to confirm your vehicle information and address in order to renew your warranty so that your coverage continues. That's a little more believable. You might not recall ever hearing anything about a warranty on your car, but you got it five years ago. Maybe they explained that when you bought it and you've just forgotten. If you aren't sure that the person contacting you is actually connected to your car dealer, or mortgage lender, or property manager, or bank like they claim to be, go ahead and hang up, and find the number or email address of your actual company or provider and give them a call directly. (Don't call back the number that just called you unless, when you find your provider's phone number, it is actually the same as the one that called you.) Ask them if whatever deal or problem you were just told about is real, and they can confirm for you whether it was really them contacting you or not. Phishing scams often come disguised as legitimate emails or messages, but they usually contain suspicious links or requests for personal information. Always verify the authenticity of a message before clicking on links or sharing details. Fake websites and pop-ups are like digital mirages, appearing real but hiding danger. Stay vigilant and trust your instincts if something feels off.

Your privacy settings are your best friends when it comes to controlling who sees your online activity. Think of them as the bouncers at your digital party, deciding who gets in and who stays out. On social media, limit who can see your posts and personal information to trusted friends. If you encounter suspicious accounts, block and report them. Regularly review app permissions to ensure they aren't overstepping boundaries. Privacy settings can change with updates to your browser or specific websites and social media sites, so check them often to maintain your desired level of privacy (*A Teens Guide to Social Media Safety*, 2024).

Navigating the internet safely is all about being aware and making smart choices. It's like having a map in that bustling digital city, guiding you past potential pitfalls and toward the best experiences. By understanding what makes your personal information valuable, creating strong passwords, recognizing scams, and using privacy settings, you're setting yourself up for a safe and enjoyable online adventure.

Don't Get Duped Online

Alright, so you're scrolling online, and boom—some wild fact pops up. "Did you know that eating 37 bananas in one sitting will make you glow in the dark?" Uh... yeah, no. The internet is a goldmine of  information, but let's be real—it's also a breeding ground for absolute nonsense. That's why fact-checking is so important. Just because something has a lot of likes or a dramatic headline doesn't mean it's true (looking at you, clickbait). Before you go telling your friends that sharks can smell fear (they can't, by the way), take a second to make sure what you're reading is legit.

So how do you do that without spending hours drowning in research? First, check where the info is coming from. Websites that end in .gov, .edu, or .org tend to be more reliable since they come from government agencies, universities, and established organizations. That random blog with neon fonts and 15 pop-up ads? Maybe not your best bet. Second, compare multiple sources. If only one sketchy website or that guy with the crazy hair on social media is saying something, but major news outlets or scientific sources aren't, chances are it's fake news. It's also good practice to research a topic using multiple different sources with different biases or political leanings to get a more well-rounded picture of an event, discovery, or debate. Since the internet and all social media sites are built around algorithms that trace your past internet activity, they're only going show you viewpoints that you already agree with unless you intentionally search for alternative viewpoints. Take the time to do that! Understanding the viewpoints of people who are different than you is so important for your personal health as a human and for the health of our society. And finally, watch out for emotional manipulation—if a post is designed to make you mad or scared without giving solid evidence, it's probably trying to mess with you. Stay sharp, question everything, and maybe don't trust the guy on TikTok saying the moon landing was filmed in someone's basement.

Recognizing and Avoiding Cyberbullying

Now back to the image of the internet as a bustling city, a vast playground, full of activity and teeming with people from all corners of the globe. While it can be a place of fun and learning, it can also harbor bullies who hide behind screens. Cyberbullying is a form of bullying that occurs online, encompassing harassment, rumor-spreading, and even impersonation. Unlike traditional bullying, it doesn't end when you leave school or close your door; it follows you home through social media, messaging apps, and even gaming platforms. These digital bullies can leave a lasting impact, causing emotional and psychological distress. They wield words and actions with the power to hurt, often leading their victims to anxiety, depression, and a reluctance to engage with electronic devices (Patchin & Hinduja, 2024).

Recognizing the signs of cyberbullying is the first step in taking back control. If someone you know suddenly changes their behavior—perhaps they become withdrawn or anxious without explanation—it might be more than just a bad day. Maybe they start to avoid their once-beloved gadgets or shy away from social interactions. These could be red flags indicating they're experiencing cyberbullying or bullying. Keep an eye out for unexplained mood changes or signs of depression. It's crucial to approach the situation with empathy and understanding, offering support rather than judgment. Sometimes, just knowing someone cares can make a world of difference.

So, how do we tackle this digital menace? First, keep your personal information under wraps. It's like keeping your diary locked—only you should have the key. Don't engage with bullies online. Responding only fuels their fire. Instead, block and report them. Most platforms have tools for this, and they're there to help you maintain a safe environment. If you're on the receiving end of hurtful messages or see something suspicious, take screenshots. This evidence can be useful if you decide to escalate the situation. Think of it as creating a digital paper trail that can help authorities or support services understand what's going on.

If you find yourself in the midst of a cyberbullying storm, don't weather it alone. Reach out to trusted adults like parents or teachers. They can offer guidance and support, providing a shoulder to lean on as you navigate the situation. Schools often have counseling services available, and these professionals are trained to help you handle what you're going through. Helplines and online support groups can also be invaluable resources, connecting you with others who understand and can offer advice. Educating your peers about the effects of cyberbullying raises awareness and fosters a community of support. It's like building a fortress of kindness, where everyone has each other's backs.

Being cyber-savvy isn't just about knowing how to navigate the web—it's about creating a safe and positive online environment. Recognizing cyberbullying and taking steps to prevent it empowers you to take control. With these tools and strategies, you can help make the internet a place where everyone feels welcome and respected.

Safe Social Media Practices

Social media platforms are like digital neighborhoods, each with their own vibe and community. Choosing the right platform is similar to picking the best neighborhood to hang out in. You want a place that feels safe, welcoming, and respects your privacy. Before signing up, do a little detective work. Research the platform's safety features—are there robust privacy controls? Can you easily report someone who's being sketchy? User reviews and feedback can be incredibly insightful. They act like Yelp reviews for social media, giving you a peek into what other users think. Understanding the terms of service and privacy policies is crucial, too. It might sound as thrilling as reading the ingredients on a cereal box, but it's important to know what you're signing up for. These documents outline how your data will be used and what rights you have, so don't skip them (*A Teens Guide to Social Media Safety*, 2024).

Once you've chosen your digital hangout, building a positive online presence is the next step. Think of your online persona as a digital version of yourself. You want it to reflect who you are in the best way possible. This means posting thoughtful and considerate content. Share things  that you're proud of and that showcase your interests and talents. Avoid sharing sensitive or inappropriate material—it's like writing a diary entry and then leaving it open for the world to read. Engaging in positive interactions with others is key, too. Spread kindness and encouragement; it's amazing how a little positivity can brighten someone's day. Remember, your online presence can have a lasting impact, so make it a good one.

Managing online friendships is another important piece of the puzzle. It's exciting to connect with new people, but it's vital to verify the identity of online friends. Make sure you know who they really are before getting too close. Setting boundaries for online communication is just as important as it is in real life. Decide what you're comfortable sharing and stick to it. Recognize red flags in online behavior, like someone asking for personal information or making you feel uncomfortable. Trust your instincts—if something feels off, it probably is. Know when to unfriend or block someone. It's okay to step back from a relationship that doesn't feel right. Your safety should always come first.

Now, let's talk about oversharing. We've all been there—caught up in the moment, posting about the awesome concert you're at or your plans for the weekend. But it's essential to think before posting. Consider who might see your post and how it could be used. Keeping certain details private, like your location or daily routines, is crucial for your safety. Understanding the permanence of online content is important, too. Once something is posted, it can be challenging to erase. It's like trying to put toothpaste back in the tube—almost impossible. Be aware of the potential consequences of oversharing. What might seem harmless now could impact you later, like when applying for a job or college.

Navigating social media safely is all about awareness and making thoughtful choices. It's about creating an online space where you feel comfortable and respected. By choosing the right platforms, building a positive online presence, managing friendships wisely, and avoiding oversharing, you're setting yourself up for a safe and enjoyable experience. Social media can be a fantastic tool for connection and creativity, so use it to showcase your best self and enjoy the digital world responsibly.

Digital Footprints and Their Impact

Picture the internet as a sandy beach. Every click, post, and search you make leaves a mark—your digital footprint. These footprints come in two flavors: active and passive. Active footprints are the ones you intentionally leave behind, like social media posts or blog entries. You're aware of these because you're consciously sharing something. On the flip side, passive footprints are more like the breadcrumbs you unknowingly scatter as you surf the web. Think search history, cookies, or data collected by apps. Even when you're just browsing, you're leaving a trail that companies can track. Understanding these footprints is like finding the map to your online self, showing where you've been and hinting at who you are.

These digital footprints can have long-lasting effects, stretching far beyond the immediate moment. Imagine applying to your dream college or that job you've always wanted. Admissions officers and employers might look at your online presence to get a sense of who you are. Your digital past could influence their decisions. It's like your online persona showing up to the interview before you do. A positive footprint could open doors, but a negative one might slam them shut. Personal reputation is another area where digital footprints weigh heavily. What you post can stick around, shaping how others perceive you. Privacy concerns also come into play. Your data can be collected, stored, and possibly misused, leading to security issues. It's like inviting strangers into your home without knowing it.

Managing your digital footprint is a bit like tidying up your room. It requires regular attention and a bit of strategy. Start by reviewing and deleting old posts that no longer represent who you are. It's like purging your closet of outdated clothes. Use privacy tools and settings to control what others can see. Being cautious about sharing personal information is key. Remember, once it's out there, it's tough to take back. Search engine privacy features can also help minimize your footprint. They're like sunglasses for your online presence, reducing the amount of data collected as you browse.

Practicing responsible digital behavior is about respecting others and making choices that reflect well on you. Always consider how your actions might affect someone else. Avoid illegal or unethical activities that could tarnish your online reputation. If you come across harmful or inappropriate content, report it. Staying informed about digital rights and responsibilities is crucial. It's like knowing the rules of the game so you can play it well. Your digital footprint is a reflection of you, so keep it clean and positive (*Advice for Teens: Manage Your Digital Footprint | UME Digital Literacy*, 2023).

As we wrap up this chapter, remember that your digital footprint is an extension of yourself in the online world. A little awareness and effort can go a long way in presenting the best version of yourself. Next, we'll explore the basics of car care, helping you hit the road with confidence and safety.

Chapter 10

Buying Your First Car

Freedom, Baby

Picture this: you're standing in front of a gleaming new car, keys in hand, feeling like you've just unlocked a level of adulthood you never knew existed. It's an exhilarating experience, but also one that comes with a thousand questions. Buying your first car isn't just about picking a color or deciding between leather or cloth seats; it's a rite of passage that requires a bit of planning and a whole lot of decision-making. Whether you're eyeing a sporty coupe or a practical sedan, there are several factors to consider before you hit the road in your new ride.

First, let's talk budget. It's easy to get swept up in the excitement of test driving a shiny new car, but it's crucial to keep your finances in check. Determine what you can comfortably afford, not just the car's sticker price but also the hidden costs—think insurance, maintenance, and gas. Experts suggest that your overall car expenses shouldn't exceed

20% of your take-home pay. Size is another important factor. Do you need a compact car for city driving or something roomier for road trips with friends? Then there's the age-old debate: two doors or four? While two-door cars can look sleek, four doors offer practicality, especially if you frequently ferry passengers. Finally, consider how weather affects driving conditions where you live. Will you be safer driving a 4WD or AWD vehicle? Or can you get away with two-wheel drive?

 As you ponder these choices, consider whether you prioritize economy or aesthetics. Fancy convertibles might turn heads, but a reliable sedan could be kinder on your wallet and more fuel-efficient. Research the longevity of the vehicle make and model you're interested in and look into common repair issues. Some brands are known for their durability, while others might have a reputation for expensive repairs. When it comes to choosing between mileage and vehicle age, it's a balancing act. A newer car with high mileage might still be a good buy if it's been well-maintained. Conversely, an older car with low mileage could be a gem if it's had a gentle life. And some vehicle brands are known for doing great even with high miles and years under their belt, as long as they've been maintained well—Honda and Toyota stand out in that arena.

Buying from a car lot offers some peace of mind, especially if you're a first-time buyer. Dealerships often provide warranties and certified pre-owned options, which can be reassuring. However, it's essential to remain vigilant. Ask about the car's history, check for any recalls, and don't hesitate to request a mechanic's inspection, especially if you're buying a used or pre-owned car. Be wary of high-pressure sales tactics that push you into a decision. Buying a car is a significant investment, so take your time to weigh your options and negotiate the best deal.

Purchasing from a private seller can be a bit like a treasure hunt. You might find a great deal, but you need to do your due diligence. Always meet in a safe, public place and bring a friend along if possible. Request to see maintenance records and have the car inspected by a trusted mechanic. Be sure to check the VIN for any past accidents or title issues. Private sales can save you money, but they also carry more risk, so proceed with caution.

Once you've found the right car, it's time to think about repairs. Whether you're buying new or used, factor in potential repair costs. Even the most reliable vehicles require maintenance. Set aside a budget for needed repairs like brake replacements or oil changes, as well as recommended maintenance like tire rotations or fluid checks. Planning for these expenses ensures that your car stays in top shape, keeping you safe on the road and preventing any unexpected breakdowns (Martin, 2025).

Car Buying Checklist

As you embark on this exciting journey, use the checklist below to guide your decision-making process. This will help ensure that you cover all your bases, from budgeting to test driving and everything in between. With the right preparation, you'll soon be cruising down the highway in your new set of wheels, ready to embrace the freedom and responsibility that comes with car ownership.

- Determine your budget, including purchase price (or

monthly loan payments), insurance, gas, and maintenance.

- Decide on the car size and 2WD vs 4WD/AWD.

- Research the makes and models you're interested in for longevity and common repair issues.

- Compare mileage versus age for potential cars.

- Test drive potential cars, focusing on comfort, handling, and performance.

- If buying from a dealer, consider dealership options and warranties, and prepare questions for the dealer. Don't forget to bargain for a better price.

- If buying privately, verify the car's history and maintenance records and arrange for an inspection by a mechanic. You can frequently also bargain down the price from a private seller, especially if you are able to pay in cash.

- Buy a car!

Now you're ready to hit the road, tires squeelin'! In the next chapter, we'll dive into keeping your wheels in top shape.

Chapter 11

Vehicle Basics

You're cruising down the highway, windows down, music blasting—total freedom. Then suddenly, a dreaded thump-thump-thump interrupts your jam session. You pull over, and there it is—a flat tire. Cue the dramatic music. But don't worry, you're about to become a tire-changing ninja. In this chapter, I'm going to guide you through the process of changing a tire, so you can get back on the road with confidence, or at least without calling your parents in a panic.

Changing a Tire Step-by-Step

First things first, preparation and safety are your best friends when dealing with a flat tire. You need a flat, stable surface—no wobbly antics here. Turn on your hazard lights to alert other drivers that something's up, and engage the parking brake to keep your car from rolling away. For extra peace of mind, place wheel wedges behind the tires. These nifty gadgets prevent any unexpected car movement. And, of course, don your safety vest and set up safety triangles if you have them. It's like marking your territory, ensuring everyone knows you're a tire-changing pro in action.

Now let's talk tools. You'll need a spare tire, a car jack, and a lug wrench. The spare tire is your knight in shining rubber, ready to roll you out of any flat situation.

The car jack is your lifting buddy, raising your car just enough to swap tires. And the lug wrench? It's your magic wand for loosening those pesky lug nuts. Don't forget your vehicle owner's manual. This little book of wonders holds all the secrets your car wants you to know, including the exact spots to place the jack.

Ready to get your hands a bit dirty? Here's the step-by-step tire-changing process. Start by slightly loosening the lug nuts while the car is still firmly on the ground. This way, you're not wrestling with the wheel when it's in the air.

Next, position the car jack under the vehicle, using the owner's manual for guidance. It's important to not just place the jack randomly. If the piece of your car you place the jack under was not made to be able to hold the weight of your vehicle, you can end up damaging your vehicle further or risk your vehicle falling down on you while you're working - both very bad scenarios. Once the jack is placed properly, crank it up until the tire is off the ground. Now you can fully remove the lug nuts and the flat tire. Out with the old, in with the new! (Make sure to keep track of where you set your lug nuts, or searching the grass on the side of the highway for a missing lug nut may become your second least favorite activity...)

 Mount the spare tire onto the hub, and hand-tighten the lug nuts. Lower the vehicle back down, and then give those lug nuts a final tightening with the lug wrench. You want them to be securely snug, but not so tight that they will be impossible for you to get off the next time your tire needs changed. Congratulations, you've just changed a tire!

But wait, there's more. After you've executed this impressive feat, a few checks are in order. Ensure the spare tire is properly inflated; a flat spare won't do you any good. (Having a tire pressure gauge on-hand in your car is a good idea.) Double-check that the lug nuts are as snug as a bug in a rug. Securely stow away your flat tire and tools, like a secret agent cleaning up after a mission. Drive cautiously until you can get your flat tire repaired or replaced, just to be safe. Spare tires are not made for long-term use or rough terrain (*How to Change a Flat Tire*, 2021).

Now, let's chat about an alternative for those who prefer less hands-on heroics: the flat repair kit. This handy kit usually includes a mini-air compressor that plugs into your car's cigarette lighter and a can of sealant to seal the leak. You'll just have to follow the directions on the package. It's not a permanent fix, but it can get you to the nearest service station without having to wrestle with lug nuts on the side of the road.

Changing a tire is a skill that builds confidence and independence. So next time you hear that telltale thump-thump, go ahead and smile, knowing you're ready for it.

Checking Oil Levels and Fluids

Imagine your car's engine like a well-oiled machine—literally. Oil is the lifeblood, keeping everything running smoothly. It lubricates engine components, reducing friction and wear, which is critical because without it, metal parts would grind against each other, leading to a noisy and very unhappy engine. But oil does more than just lubricate. It helps regulate the engine's temperature, ensuring things don't get too heated under the hood. Plus, it carries away contaminants and tiny particles, keeping the engine clean and efficient. So, maintaining proper oil levels isn't just a good idea; it's necessary for your car's health and longevity (*How important is an oil change?*, 2024).

Checking your car's oil levels is a straightforward process, but it's one of those tasks that makes you feel like a real car whisperer. Start by parking your car on a level surface and turning off the engine. You'll need to wait 15 minutes or so for the engine to cool down if

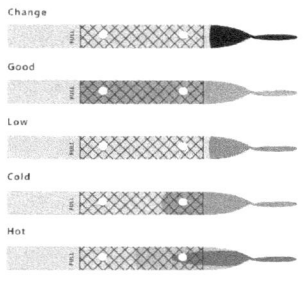

you've been driving recently; nobody wants oil splattering everywhere like some high-octane cooking show. Next, pop the hood and locate the dipstick—usually a bright yellow or orange ring. As with all things vehicle, your car's manual is a great place to get help if you're not sure where to find your oil dipstick. Remove it and wipe it clean with a paper towel to get an accurate reading. Then, insert it back into the tube and pull it out again. Now, check where the oil mark falls between the min and max lines (or sometimes they're just dots). If it's low, especially if it's below the minimum line, your engine is thirsty.

Adding oil is easy, but it's not a free-for-all. Start by choosing the right type of oil for your car. Your owner's manual will tell you what's best, but if you're unsure, ask at your local auto parts store. If you give them your car's year, make, and model, they can find what you need. Use a funnel to avoid spills, and pour in a little at a time. (Keeping a dedicated oil funnel in your car for this purpose is helpful; don't use the same funnel for other car fluids because mixing car fluids can be dangerous.) Keep checking the level with the dipstick to ensure you're not overfilling, because too much oil can be just as problematic as too little. This process is like topping off a drink—slowly and carefully to avoid overflow.

If the oil on your dipstick when you check your oil is very dark in color instead of mostly clear, it's time for an oil change. Your car's manual can also tell you about how often you should plan to change your oil based on how many miles your car has been driven since the last oil change. Changing your car's oil is a bit more involved than just topping off, but totally doable if you're up for it. First, gather your materials: a car jack, four jack stands, an oil filter, an oil drain pan, a regular wrench, an oil filter wrench, some plastic gloves, and 4-6 quarts of new oil. Safety first—make sure your car is elevated properly with a jack and jack stands. Again, check your car's manual for proper jack placement. Unlike with changing a tire, you're going to need to use the jack more than once, because you're lifting the whole car, not just one corner. Use the jack to lift each corner one at a time—enough to place a jack stand under each corner. The jack stands will stay in place throughout the full oil changing process, and they are what should be holding your car's weight, not the jack itself. Make sure they are properly locked! Consult the manual or instructions that came with your jack stands to make sure you have them properly locked before you crawl under your car. Put your gloves on for the rest of the procedure. It gets messy pretty fast.

Locate your oil pan and oil filter beneath the car. The oil filter is a round cylinder about as big around as a water bottle. The large metal container next to it is your oil pan, and coming out of the oil pan somewhere near the filter will be a small protrusion from the pan with a metal bolt on it. This is the drain plug.

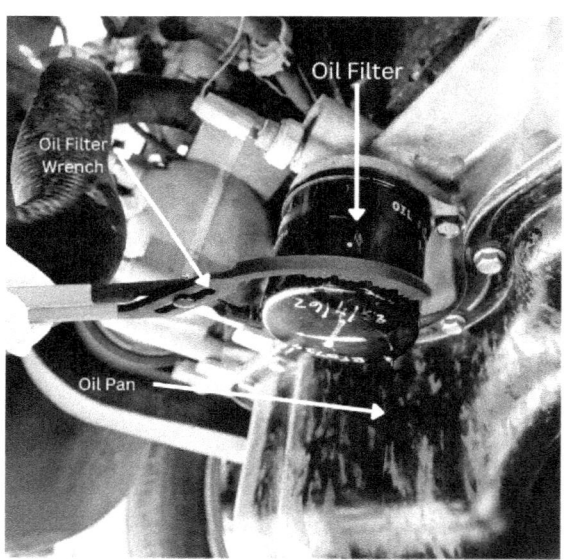

Oil Drain Plug

Situate your oil drain pan where it will catch the oil that will pour out of the drain plug (keeping in mind the oil will come out with gusto at first, so maybe place the plan slightly further forward instead of directly under the drain to start). Drain the old oil by removing the drain plug, letting gravity do its thing into the pan below. Then, remove the old oil filter by unscrewing it with an oil filter wrench (found at any auto parts store)—be prepared for a bit more oil to spill out here. Before screwing in the new filter, use your gloved finger to spread a bit of oil on the rubber gasket at the top of the new filter. This helps ensure a tighter seal when you screw it in. Now install the new filter by screwing it in tightly—first by hand, then finishing with a 1/8 turn with the oil filter wrench. Now replace the drain plug snuggly (again, first by hand then with a 1/8 to 1/4 turn with a wrench), and add fresh oil through the oil cap under your hood the same way you did when you checked oil levels previously, checking for leaks as you go. An average-sized car will take 4-6 quarts of oil normally, but check out that handy dandy vehicle manual again for how much your specific car needs. It's a messy job, but there's something satisfying about knowing you've given your car a new lease on life.

While you're under the hood, it's a good time to check other fluids too. Automatic transmission fluid (ATF) is vital for shifting gears smoothly. Park the car on a level surface, with the engine still running and hot. If you just started your car, you'll want to let it run for 15 minutes or so to make sure the engine is hot and shift through the different gears a couple times to get transmission fluid running through the system. Locate the ATF dipstick. It's usually marked, and your owner's manual can guide you if you're unsure. Pull it out, wipe it clean with a paper towel, reinsert it, and check the level. Just like with the oil, there will be a line or dot to mark the minimum and the maximum fill capacity. Add ATF if needed, using a transmission fluid funnel to prevent spills. (Don't use the same funnel you use for oil. Getting leftover oil into your transmission fluid is a big problem.) Remember, a little at a time and reinsert the dipstick along the way to check to avoid overfilling.

Don't forget the brake fluid, which is crucial for stopping power. The reservoir is usually clear, so you can see the level without opening it. If it's low, top it off to the max line with the correct type of fluid. (Check your manual.) Power steering fluid is another one to watch, ensuring your steering wheel moves smoothly without any hitches. It will also be a clear reservoir so that you can see the fill level easily. Coolant keeps your vehicle from overheating. Check that it is between the min and max lines on the reservoir as well. Lastly, check the windshield washer fluid. It might seem minor, but having a clean windshield is essential for visibility, especially in bad weather. Again, your owner's manual for your vehicle is like the secret treasure map to help you find where all of these gems are hiding. Keeping these fluids in check ensures your car remains in peak condition, ready to take on any adventure you throw its way.

If you're not into the DIY method with your car, many auto parts stores will top off fluids for you for free if you buy your fluids from them. Some of the big chains are O'Reilley's Auto Parts, AutoZone, and Advanced Auto. Go in and have them help you find the right fluids for your car's make and model, and if they don't immediately offer when you make your purchase, just ask if they offer fluid refill services for free. The answer should be "Yes!" (Pro tip: these places will also usually replace windshield wipers, car batteries, and headlights for free if you purchase the parts from them. It's way cheaper than going to a mechanic and way faster than watching 7 Youtube videos before you have the nerve to try it yourself!) As with all things adulting, don't be afraid to ask other people for help. If it's someone else's job to know about cars, they're a good person to ask when you're trying to figure out your car.

Understanding Dashboard Warning Lights

This time, you're driving down the highway, feeling like the king or queen of the road, when suddenly, out of nowhere, a little light starts blinking on your dashboard. It's like your car's way of saying, "Hey, we need to talk." These dashboard warning lights are your vehicle's direct line of communication, each with its unique message. Let's break down the most common lights you might encounter. First up is the infamous check engine light. It could mean anything from a loose gas cap to something really serious under the hood. Then there's the oil pressure warning light, which might be your engine's way of begging for a little more oil. The battery warning light is another common one, indicating possible issues with the battery, wiring, or alternator. And don't forget the tire pressure monitoring system (TPMS) light. This light is your friendly reminder that your tires might need a bit more air to keep rolling smoothly.

Now, what do you do when one of these lights decides to crash your driving party? The owner's manual is your secret decoder ring. It will help you understand what each light means and what steps to take next. If the light is red, it's screaming for immediate attention. Pull over safely and address the issue as soon as possible. Yellow or orange lights are more like a gentle nudge, suggesting you schedule a service appointment to prevent bigger problems down the road. But don't ignore them, because they're like ticking time bombs that could lead to more severe issues if left unchecked. You can also stop at most auto repair supply stores (like the ones mentioned in the section above), and they can use a computer to read your car's warning codes and tell you more precisely what the problem is for free (Kurczewski, 2021).

Keeping your car healthy is like maintaining a good diet—it requires regular attention and care. Regular maintenance checks are your car's version of medical check-ups, ensuring everything is running smoothly. Keep up with oil changes and fluid levels to avoid any surprises that might trigger those pesky lights. Inspect your tires and brakes routinely, as they are crucial for your safety and performance. And always be on the lookout for unusual sounds or changes in how your car handles. These subtle hints can be tell-tale signs of underlying issues.

Sometimes, though, your car might throw a curveball that even the most attentive drivers can't catch. That's when it's time to call in the pros. If a warning light persists or keeps coming back despite your best efforts, it's time to consult a professional mechanic. Unusual smells or smoke are red flags that something more serious is brewing under the hood. If you ever see or smell smoke coming from under your hood, pull over immediately, exit your vehicle and get away to a safe distance, and call for help. Noticeable changes in how your vehicle drives, like pulling to one side or a weird noise from the engine, are also cues to seek expert help. Sometimes, even if you're a car enthusiast with a knack for diagnosing issues, you might find yourself stumped.

That's when it's best to let a skilled mechanic take over. Check internet reviews to find a trustworthy mechanic with good prices. Once you've found a mechanic that you like who has proven they do good, honest work, stick with them. They can help you keep track of your car's regular maintenance needs and send you reminders when certain services are due to keep your car running in good condition.

Understanding dashboard warning lights is like learning your car's language. It helps you keep your vehicle in top shape and ensures you're ready to address issues before they escalate. With this knowledge in your toolkit, you can drive with confidence, knowing you're in tune with every beep and blink your car has to offer.

Interactive Element: Operation "Make the Mechanic Less Scary"

Whether you have a go-to mechanic already or not, here's a little practice challenge just to get your feet wet. Look up mechanic shops near you, and compare reviews for them online. Pick two that have good ratings and reviews, and then give them each a call and ask for a quote for some kind of vehicle maintenance request (such as replacing brake pads, doing a transmission flush, or giving your car a pre-road-trip checkup). They will ask you for your car's year, make, and model to give you an accurate quote. Make sure to ask them what all the price they have quoted you for includes, and have them explain any procedures that you don't understand. Ask whether they offer any complimentary services, such as free drop-off and pick-up at a nearby location while your car is in the shop, or an app where you can see pictures and mechanic's notes for any problems they find with your vehicle to reference later. Have a notepad with you while you make the call and jot down the answers each mechanic gives you so that you can compare afterward. Once all your questions have been answered, thank them for their time and let them know you might be in touch later to schedule an appointment. Now you can compare your notes from the two calls and see which mechanic sounds like the best option for when you actually need that service done for your vehicle. And voila! Calling a mechanic isn't so scary now.

Basic Car Maintenance and Safety Tips

Owning a car is a bit like having a pet. It needs regular attention, a little TLC, and yes, the occasional check-up to keep it purring smoothly. One of the simplest yet most crucial tasks is checking the tire pressure regularly. Properly inflated tires are not just about saving gas or extending tire life; they're also a safety feature. Underinflated tires can lead to poor handling, increased wear, and even blowouts. Checking your car tire pressure with a gauge is super easy and only takes a couple of minutes. First, grab your tire pressure gauge (digital or the old-school stick kind works). Look in your car's owner manual or on the sticker inside the driver's door to find the recommended tire pressure—this is the number you're aiming for, usually listed in PSI (pounds per square inch). Remove the cap from the tire's valve stem (the little nozzle sticking out of the wheel), press the gauge firmly onto the valve, pull it back off, and check the reading. If it's too low, you'll need to add air, and if it's too high, you can let some air out by pressing the pin inside the valve. If you need to add air, head to a local gas station. Most gas stations have tire fill stations for a small fee or even for free. Follow the directions on the fill station to bring your tire up to the proper PSI reading. Once you're done, put the cap back on, and you're good to go!

While you're at it, take a peek at your car's air filters. These little guys are the lungs of your car, and a clogged filter can choke your engine, reducing efficiency. Checking and replacing your car's air filter is super simple and can make a big difference in how your car runs. First, pop the hood and locate the air filter—it's usually in a rectangular or round plastic box near the engine. Check your owner's manual if you're not sure where to look. Open the air filter housing (you might need to unsnap clips or remove a few screws) and pull out the filter. Hold it up to the light—if it looks dirty, clogged, or you can't see much light through it, it's time for a new one. Take the old filter to an auto parts store to grab the right replacement, or look up your car's model to buy the right size. To replace it, just pop the new filter in the same way the old one came out, close the housing, and you're ready to roll. It's a quick job that'll keep your engine breathing easy and running more efficiently. (And again, many auto part stores will replace it for you in the parking lot immediately at no cost if you buy your new one from them.) You can also check and change out your cabin air filter using the same method. Check your manual for exact location, but typically it can be accessed through the glove compartment or somewhere in that area.

Check fluid levels regularly and top them off as necessary like we talked about earlier. Lastly, inspect those wiper blades and lights. Clear visibility and functioning lights are your first line of defense on the road.

As the seasons change, so should your car care routine. Winter can be tough on vehicles, so make sure to check antifreeze levels to prevent your engine from freezing and cracking. Consider switching to winter tires if you live in an area prone to snow and ice; they provide better traction and safety. Inspect the heating system, and don't forget to run the A/C occasionally to keep the seals lubricated. In summer, focus on the air conditioning to ensure it's ready to combat the heat, inspect tire pressure frequently as it tends to fluctuate with temperature changes, and make sure your coolant levels are adequate to prevent overheating. Each season brings its challenges, but with a little preparation, your car will be ready to face them all (Travelers, 2023).

Before you even hit the road, a few safety checks can make all the difference. Ensure all lights, including headlights, brake lights, and indicators, are functioning properly. They're your car's way of communicating with the world around you. Adjust mirrors for maximum visibility, and make sure seat belts are in good condition and worn properly by everyone in the car. It might sound simple, but these checks are key to a safe journey for everyone.

 Being prepared for car emergencies is like having an umbrella on a sunny day—it's better to have it and not need it than to need it and not have it. Keep an emergency kit in your car with essentials like a first aid kit, flashlight, jumper cables, safety triangles, and a safety vest. Keeping some extra oil and wiper fluid can also be helpful in a pinch. If you live where winter weather is a thing, add a winter emergency kit with a safety blanket, non-perishable food, and water. Keep contact information for roadside assistance handy, and always have important documents like insurance and registration accessible.

Knowing how to jump-start a car is a lifesaver for dead batteries, so familiarize yourself with the process. It's easy once you know the steps, and it'll save you when your car won't start! First, you'll need jumper cables and a second car with a working battery. Park the cars close but not touching, and turn both cars off. Now pay attention because the order of operations here is important! Connect the red cable clamp to the *dead* battery's positive (+) terminal, then connect the other red clamp to the positive terminal on the *working* car's battery. Next, connect the black cable clamp to the *working* battery's negative (-) terminal, and clip the other black clamp to an unpainted metal surface on the *dead* car, like a bolt or the engine block—this grounds it safely. (Avoid connecting it to the dead battery's negative terminal directly because there's a possibility this can cause a spark and potentially light hydrogen fumes from your vehicle on fire—kablooey! For the same reason—no kablooies wanted—make sure not to touch the jumper cable ends to each other or to any other random metal surfaces while you're going through the process of connecting and disconnecting everything. Even if it doesn't cause a spark, it can easily ruin your battery. *Precision is key here.*)

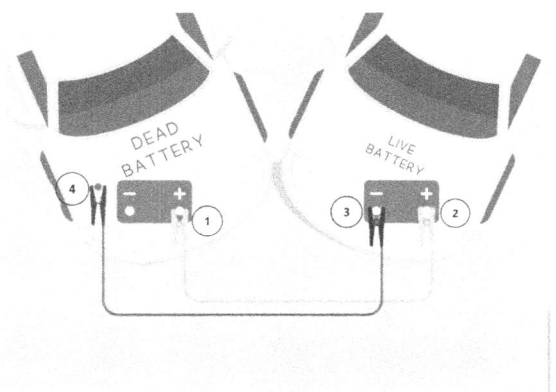

Start the working car and let it run for a minute or two, then try starting the dead car. Once it starts, disconnect the cables in *reverse* order (black clamp on the metal ground first, then the rest in the opposite order you connected them in the first place). Let your car run for a while to recharge its battery the rest of the way (AAA, 2023).

Car maintenance might seem like a hassle, but it's your ticket to worry-free driving. By staying on top of these tasks, you're not just caring for your car; you're ensuring your safety and the safety of others on the road. This chapter is your guide to keeping your vehicle in peak condition, ready for any adventure that comes your way.

Chapter 12

Life After High School

N ext to getting your first car and moving into your own place, deciding what direction you want to head after high school is one of the most exciting decisions of your launch into adulthood. But it's not a simple decision, and sometimes it can feel paralyzing because of how many different options there are. But don't worry, this book is here to shed some light on that dark abyss for you.

Let's start with trade school, often the road less traveled but definitely worth considering. Trade schools offer programs that are shorter and more focused than a traditional college degree, usually lasting one to two years. These programs specialize in fields like healthcare, first responders, technolo-

gy, mechanics, and construction, giving you hands-on experience right from the start. This practical approach means you can jump into the workforce sooner and start earning a decent wage. Many trades are in high demand, so job opportunities are plentiful and wages are often good.

But, like everything in life, trade schools have their downsides. The skills you learn are specific to the trade you choose, which means your career options are somewhat limited. If you decide to switch fields later, you might find yourself starting from scratch. Additionally, while trades can offer good wages, the income potential might not reach the heights of some careers that require a four-year degree. And let's not forget, some trades come with health risks—working as an electrician or plumber isn't without its hazards. Even so, if you're itching to get into the workforce and start earning good wages—especially if you like working with your hands or physically active jobs—trade school might be a great fit for you (Indeed Editorial Team, 2025).

Now, let's wander over to the college path. Ah, college—the land of late-night study sessions, campus events, and lifelong friendships. Many graduates reminisce fondly about their college years, not just for the education but for the experiences. College opens doors to careers like teaching, law, and medicine, where a bachelor's degree is a must. Over time, college graduates often find that their income potential is higher compared to non-graduates (key word: *potential*). However, the journey to that diploma isn't short. Pursuing a college degree requires more time and often more money. The cost of tuition can be daunting, and many students find themselves saddled with debt upon graduation. There's also the issue of a competitive job market. With so many college graduates, you might need a master's or even a Ph.D. to stand out. Plus, it's not uncommon for students to change their majors multiple times, leading to extra years in school and additional expenses. In fact, about a third of students change their major at least once, with some switching three times or more (National Center for Education Statistics, 2017).

If you're considering college, don't be swayed solely by prestige. A high-priced degree doesn't always equal higher pay. Many employers care more about your skills and experience than the name on your diploma. Con-sider starting at a community college or a state university to save money. A gap year or two could also be beneficial, giving you time to explore your interests and solidify your field of study before committing to a major.

Next up, there's the entrepre-neurial route—a path paved with creativity and independence. If this route interests you, consider your skills and interests and how you could monetize them to meet

a public need or want. ("Monetize" being the Swedish word for "make it make me some muuuula." Just kidding, but also, yes.) Do you have an eye for design and skills in using graphic design platforms? Start marketing yourself as a graphic artist. Do you love to cook? Come up with a business plan for a food truck. Are your Instagram videos making people forget to keep scrolling? Start selling your expertise to businesses. Artist, self-published writer, dog trainer, professional organizer—the opportunities are endless. Being your own boss allows for immense freedom and the potential for significant earnings. You can start your venture quickly, without the need for formal education or a mountain of student loans. However, entrepreneurship isn't a guaranteed goldmine. The road is fraught with challenges and often requires initial financial investment and has a steep learning curve. You need a high level of self-motivation and resilience to weather the ups and downs of running a business or being self-employed, and you have to be dedicated to doing the research to find out how to make your business work. It's also a good idea to find someone who would be willing to mentor you as you start your entrepreneurial journey. Find someone who has done it before, and learn from them! Even if they haven't necessarily started a business in the same field as you, they can still give you valuable insight into all those sneaky parts of running a business that nobody likes to think about (like licenses, marketing, accounting, and business taxes... *shudder*.) And don't be afraid to fail the first time (or seven times) you try! Figure out what went wrong, save up some money, and try it again a different way. It's okay for it to be a process.

Finally, there's the red-headed stepchild no one seems to talk about—getting a job after high school. Lots of people are able to find jobs that pay them a comfortable living wage and that they enjoy without ever getting any kind of degree or taking on a business startup venture. Better yet, doing a working holiday in another country for a year or two exposes you to learning you could never get in a school or in the context of your own culture. Some of my favorite jobs have been jobs that I didn't need a degree for and found because I wasn't set on getting established in a specific career. I've been a supplies coordinator at a nonprofit in the Middle East, a teacher's aide and substitute teacher for a K-8 charter school, and a pastry chef and baker for a dude ranch in the Rocky Mountains of Colorado—all with nothing to recommend me for the jobs but a good work ethic, strong references and letters of recommendation, and a willingness to learn. (And these are just the ones I've had that I really enjoyed; I've gotten to try a lot more!) In fact, one of these jobs advertised that a Bachelor's degree was required, and I applied anyway and got the job. As we talked about in Chapter 6, sell your skills and experience. Often employers are happy to train someone from the ground up who has a good work ethic, good character, and is willing to learn instead of trying to retrain someone fresh out of college who thinks they know everything already.

That being said, finding a job you really enjoy and that pays you what you'd like to make is usually a journey. If you go this route, don't expect your first job straight out of high school to be your dream job. Often, you will need to work some jobs you don't enjoy for a while to gain experience, get a reputation for being a good worker, and network to find opportunities you're interested in. Don't worry if you can't find a job that fits you well right away. Give each job you have an honest try, and use it as a stepping stone to help you learn what you enjoy, what you're really good at, and what you want out of a workplace culture. Over time, you'll get better and better at spotting job opportunities that will fit you well, and you'll grow your skill sets and experience to be able to pursue those new opportunities when they arise. And that's true regardless of which track you take after high school.

Choosing between trade school, college, entrepreneurship, or getting a job after high school is a deeply personal decision. Each path offers unique opportunities and challenges, and it's important to weigh them carefully. Consider your interests, financial situation, and long-term goals as you stand at this crossroads. And remember, the direction you go right after high school doesn't have to be the direction you go for the rest of your life. Let me take some of that pressure off right now—it's okay to try something and decide it's not working for you.

Just be sure to give yourself enough time to conquer the learning curve before you make your assessment of whether it fits you; everything new is hard in the beginning. (Heck, you can even decide to go to college for the first time as a middle-aged adult if you want! You'd be surprised how com-  mon that actually is.) There's no "one size fits all" when it comes to your future. The best path is the one that aligns with who you are and what you want out of life, and it takes time to figure those things out.

Chapter 13

So You're Thinking About Renting Your First Place?

Congratulations! You're about to level up to full-on adulting. Renting your first apartment or house is a rite of passage, like learning to parallel park or realizing that you *actually* have to pay for your own toothpaste now. But before you dive into the world of leases, deposits, and internet bills, let's break it all down so you're not blindsided by the fine print or stuck in a sketchy neighborhood with a leaky ceiling.

Renting vs. Buying: The Big Picture

First off, let's clear something up: Renting and buying are two totally different vibes. Renting is like dating—you're committing, but not forever. Buying? That's marriage, my friend. It's a long-term relationship with a mortgage and property taxes. Renting is usually better for those just starting out, saving for the future, or unsure where they'll be in a year or two. Buying can make sense when you've got some financial stability, want to build equity, and are ready to settle down for a while. For now, we'll focus on renting—the starter pack for independent living.

Step 1: Finding the Perfect Pad

Budget Basics

Before you even start looking, figure out how much you can spend. A good rule of thumb? Keep your rent at around 30% of your monthly income. That leaves room for groceries, gas, and the occasional taco binge. Don't forget to factor in additional living costs, like utilities, internet, and trash services.

Tools of the Trade

Start your search online with apps and websites like Zillow, Apartments.com, or even Facebook Marketplace. Local community boards and word-of-mouth can also score you great finds. Want a roommate? Try platforms like Roomster or ask your most responsible friend.

Neighborhood Vibes

 Scout out the area. Is it safe? Are there grocery stores, public transport, or your favorite coffee shop nearby? Walk around during the day *and* at night to get a feel for the vibe. Trust your gut—if it feels sketchy, it probably is.

Step 2: The Walk-Through

Once you've narrowed it down, it's time to schedule a walk-through. This is like a first date with your potential new home. You're looking for red flags and deal breakers. Here's your checklist:

Things to check:

- **Water pressure:** Turn on the faucets and flush the toilet. No one wants to live with a sad drizzle of a shower.

- **Appliances:** If the unit comes with a fridge, oven, or washer/dryer, make sure they work.

- **Outlets:** Bring your phone charger and test a few plugs.

- **Doors and windows:** Make sure they open, close, and lock properly.

- **Leaks and pests:** Look under sinks and around baseboards for signs of water damage, mold, or creepy crawlies. A fresh coat of paint might hide a multitude of sins, so be thorough in your inspection. Discoloration in wood or beneath paint is a tell-tale sign that something might be going on.

Questions to ask the landlord:

- What utilities are included?

- What's the average utility bill?

- How is maintenance handled?

- Are pets allowed? (More on that in a bit.)

- What's the parking situation?

- What yard care (if any) would I be responsible for?

- Are laundry facilities provided in the apartment? Or shared by the complex? Or not provided at all?

Red flags:

- Unresponsive landlord or property manager.

- Strong smells (mold, mildew, or mystery odors).

- Lots of repairs that "will be fixed soon."

Step 3: Sealing the Deal

The Application Process

Found a place you love? Time to apply. You'll likely need:

- A filled-out application (usually online).

- Proof of income (pay stubs, bank statements, or a job offer letter or contract).

- A co-signer if you're short on credit history. (This is usually a friend or family member who agrees to be financially liable if you don't pay your rent like you're supposed to. Don't ruin your relationship with this person—pay your rent on time!)

- A small application fee.

Deposits and Fees

- **Security deposit:** This is usually equal to one month's rent and acts as insurance for the landlord. You'll (hopefully) get it back when you move out, as long as you don't trash the place. Your lease should have details about what will be expected of you on move-out in order to get your full security deposit back.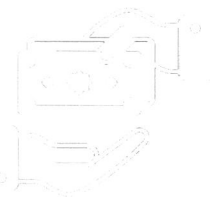

- **Pet deposit:** If you've got a furry friend, you might need to pay extra upfront. Like your security deposit, this should be returned to you on move-out if your pet hasn't caused any damages.

- **Pet rent:** Yes, your dog may cost you monthly rent, too. Because landlords can't resist making Fido pay his share.

The Lease

A lease is a legal document that spells out all the rules of living there. Read it. Seriously. Pay attention to:

- Rent amount and due date.

- Lease length (month-to-month, 6 months, a full year, etc.).

- Rules about breaking the lease early.

- Additional fees (late fees, cleaning fees, etc.).

Pro tip: Breaking a lease early can cost you big time. Make sure you're ready to commit before you sign on the dotted line. While this type of serious commitment might make a month-to-month lease seem more attractive than signing a lease for 6 months or a year, be aware that as each lease period ends, your landlord is free to change the terms of the lease before offering you a renewal. This means that if you sign a 6 month lease just to try it out so that you are free to move at the end of 6 months if you want, your landlord is also free to raise the rent at the end of 6 months if you decide you want to stay and extend your lease. The longer the lease term, the longer you have a guaranteed rent cost that can't be raised until the expiration of the current lease. Longer leases create more stability for both you and your landlord.

Leases are often written with a lot of legal jargon, so don't be afraid to ask the property manager or landlord to explain it to you in plain language so you understand exactly what you're agreeing to. You're signing up for a commitment, so make sure you're comfortable with all the details (Blake et al., 2024).

Step 4: Move-In Day

Set Up Essentials

- **Utilities:** Water, electricity, and gas—call the provider and transfer them to your name. Most cities just have one primary provider, so you won't need to do any shopping around. All you'll need is the address of your new place, the date that you are moving in, and card or bank information for where you want to be billed.

- **Internet:** Shop around for deals. Some providers will even waive installation fees for new customers. Also, read company reviews online. Some providers offer great deals initially but are notorious for terrible customer service. Figure out what is most important to you and find what fits you best. Getting internet fully operational at a new place can sometimes take up to a couple weeks, depending on the company you choose, so look into this before moving day.

- **Trash and recycling:** Depending on where you live, this might be part of your rent or something you'll need to arrange separately. Again, shop around for deals and read customer reviews online to make your choice. It's as simple as searching "trash services in my city." They'll need your address and payment information, and then they will drop off your dumpsters for you. Pay attention to which day of the week your company comes to collect trash so that you can roll your dumpster to the curb the night before.

Documentation

 Walk around like a detective and take photos of every room when you officially get your keys, especially take pictures of any pre-existing damages. Send these to your landlord so you don't get blamed (and charged) for them later. Also, be careful when moving furniture in. Scratches on floors or chips on wall corners are the kinds of things that the landlord can retain money from your security deposit for later if they need to make repairs when you move out.

Step 5: Living Your Best Rental Life

Communication is Key

If something breaks, let your landlord or property manager know ASAP. Most maintenance issues (leaks, heating issues, structural problems) are their responsibility. But things like changing lightbulbs? That's on you. If disputes arise with your landlord, communication is key. Address concerns promptly and document everything in writing. If your landlord verbally gives you permission to do something, ask them to write you an email or a signed written note stating that they've given you that permission. That way, if there are ever issues that need to be addressed on a legal level, you will have evidence in writing of any promises your landlord has made or any agreements that you made. If issues persist, knowing when and how to seek legal advice can be invaluable. It's a balance between knowing your rights and fulfilling your duties, ensuring a smooth and pleasant rental experience.

Know Your Rights

As a tenant, you have rights and responsibilities. You're entitled to privacy and a habitable living environment, free from health hazards and with functioning utilities. But you also have responsibilities, like paying rent on time and keeping the property in good condition. Look up renter's rights in your state. These laws protect you from unfair practices like sudden evictions or unsafe living conditions.

Saving Money

Are you in an area where the cost of living is really high? Here's some ways to conserve funds as you move into the world of paying rent:

- Split costs with roommates. Even though living by yourself might sound like the dream, splitting rent with a trustworthy roommate can not only cut living costs in half, but also be a ton of fun on those nights where you don't have any plans.

- Conserve energy. You're the one paying for all your utilities now, so if you want to pay less, use less water, electricity, and heat. Turn off lights when you're not in the room. Only run the dishwasher when it's full. Turn your heat down at night and when you're gone at work during the day.

- Cook at home instead of eating out. This helps no matter where you're living. Food is one of the biggest parts of overall living expenses in many areas, so eating cheaper at home may help you be able to afford rent in a nicer area.

Final Thoughts

Renting your first place is a big step, but it doesn't have to be overwhelming. Do your research, ask the right questions, and take your time finding a space that feels like home. And remember: It's okay if  your first apartment isn't perfect. It's a starting point, not the finish line. You've got this!

Chapter 14

Advanced Personal Finance

axes are the invisible hands that touch nearly every aspect of our lives without us even realizing it. They keep the wheels of society turning, funding everything from schools to roads. However, when you're just starting out on your financial journey, figuring them out can seem as perplexing as using the Rosetta Stone to learn to read Egyptian hieroglyphs. This chapter is your guide to navigating the world of taxes, turning those cryptic forms into something you can easily decipher.

Let's start with the different types of taxes you might encounter. Imagine taxes as the various toll booths on the road of life. First up, we have federal and state income taxes. Think of these as the main gatekeepers. The federal government collects income taxes

based on your earnings, applying different rates depending on how much you make. Meanwhile, state income taxes vary depending on where you live, with some states skipping this toll booth altogether (lucky you if you live in one of those!). Next, there's the sales tax, adding a bit of extra to most of your purchases. It's that hidden fee that sneaks onto your receipts, funding state and local projects. Then there's property tax, which applies to real estate you own, supporting schools and local services. Lastly, payroll taxes, such as Social Security and Medicare, are like the backstage crew ensuring your future self is taken care of in retirement. These are deducted from your paycheck by your employer before you actually get paid — a small price today that hopefully gives peace of mind tomorrow.

Speaking of paychecks, let's delve into the art of reading a pay stub. If you've ever wondered why your paycheck is smaller than expected, your pay stub holds the answers. Let's look at the different terms and abbreviations you might find on your pay stub. Start with *gross pay* —that's the disgusting part of your income. Just kidding. Gross pay is the total amount you earn before any deductions. It's the big number on your paycheck that makes you smile... until you see the deductions. Mandatory deductions include federal and state income taxes, Social Security, and Medicare. Voluntary deductions, like health insurance or retirement contributions, are optional and can vary based on your choices when you get hired. Be sure to ask your HR manager questions when you sign your onboarding paperwork if you aren't sure what your options are or what some terms mean. Once all your deductions are subtracted, you're left with *net pay*, the actual amount you take home. Pay stubs also include abbreviations like FICA (Federal Insurance Contributions Act) and FED (federal taxes), which might sound like secret codes but are just standard terms for taxes and withholdings. Finally, keep an eye on the year-to-date totals, which summarize all your earnings and deductions for the year, giving you a snapshot of your financial journey (Bank of America, 2024). Check out the QR code for a visual sample of a paycheck stub:

 Now, on to the grand adventure of filing taxes for the first time. Filing taxes might seem daunting, but with a little guidance, it's a manageable feat. Start by determining your filing status. Are you single, married, or perhaps a head of household (meaning you are unmarried and have children who are dependent on your income)? Your status affects your tax rates and the forms you'll need. Gather necessary documents like W-2s from employers and 1099 forms for any freelance gigs or investments. Typically, all of these forms will be sent to you by your employer, bank, etc. either electronically or by mail sometime during the month of January. (Unless you made less than $600 from an employer during the year; in that case, they don't have to send you a W-2, but you do still have to report that income on your taxes.) These documents are your golden tickets to accurately reporting your income.

Next, consider using tax software or hiring a tax professional to navigate the process. Software can simplify calculations and ensure you don't miss any credits or deductions. There are lots of different options, and a quick online search can allow you to compare the costs and user reviews of different software, or different tax professionals and their rates and reviews.  Filing deadlines are crucial too. The deadline for non-business owners is typically April 15th, and late filing can result in serious penalties—Uncle Sam is a stickler about accuracy and promptness on taxes. Scan the QR code for a sneak-peek at a W-2 form:

 Let's talk about deductions and credits, the secret weapons to reduce your taxable income. We used the term "deductions" earlier when we talked about your paystub. In that case, deductions were money being taken away from your gross pay, reducing your overall take-home pay. However, deductions during the tax process reduce how much you have to pay in taxes, making them way more exciting than paystub deductions! The standard deduction is a flat amount you can subtract from your income, simplifying the process for many. If you have specific expenses for a business or student expenses, itemized deductions might be the way to go, allowing you to deduct things like mortgage interest or medical expenses. For students, education-related credits like the American Opportunity Credit can offset tuition costs, making college a bit more affordable. The Earned Income Tax Credit (EITC) helps lower-income individuals and families, putting money back in their pockets. If you're paying off student loans, the student loan interest deduction can ease the burden by reducing your taxable income. These deductions and credits are like little financial boosts, helping you keep more of your hard-earned money (Buttonow, 2020). If you use online tax software or a tax professional, they should ask you questions about all of these things and help you determine whether getting the standard deduction is best for you or if you would benefit from an itemized deduction that has you document all the little details of your financial story.

Start Now: The Tax Filing Pregame

One of the best ways to save yourself a lot of headache when tax time comes is to keep your important paperwork organized throughout the year. Treat yourself to some sanity and buy an accordion file organizer.

It's important to keep tax documents for three years after filing so that
you can have them for reference if the
IRS decides to audit you at some point
for a past year's taxes. (Auditing means
that they conduct an official investiga-

tion of your accounts and finances to make sure that you haven't been
up to any funny business with your taxes.) So in your new organizer,
create labels for separate years for the next three years. Within each
year, label a folder for tax documents (like W-2s), a folder for receipts
from business related expenses that you could use for deductions, a
folder for house documents, a folder for vehicle documents, a folder
for medical documents, a folder for school documents (not homework—financial documents), a folder for travel documents, and any
other categories that you think will help you keep track of important documents throughout the year. Now, put all your important
documents in the correct folders! If you do this as you get important
paperwork throughout the year, it will save you tons of time and
energy when tax season arrives. You'll know exactly where to look to
find everything you might need.

Managing and Avoiding Debt

Picture debt as a double-edged sword—handy when wielded wisely,
but very hazardous if mishandled. Understanding its various forms
can help you navigate through financial decisions with confidence.
Let's start with the ever-popular credit card debt. It's like a tempting
buffet where you can have your cake and eat it too, but remember,
there's always a bill at the end. Credit cards offer convenience and
rewards, but if not paid off quickly, interest can balloon, turning a

small purchase into a financial mountain. Then there are student loans, often considered a rite of passage for many pursuing higher education. While they open doors to opportunities, they also need careful consideration as they can linger much longer than a bad haircut. Next, auto loans come into play when you need a set of wheels. They're generally structured with a fixed repayment plan, but it's important to avoid borrowing more than you can comfortably pay back. Mortgages, the behemoth of loans, allow you to own property but require a (very) long-term commitment. Each type of debt serves a different purpose, and understanding their implications can help you make informed choices.

Managing existing debt is like taming a wild beast—it requires strategy and discipline. Start by creating a debt repayment plan. List all your debts, from the smallest to the largest, and decide how much you can realistically pay each month. Prioritizing high-interest debt is crucial, as it can exponentially reproduce if left unchecked.

(You may recall from Chapter 1, interest is a percentage of the amount you take out on a loan or pay with a credit card, which is added onto your bill later when you repay the loan. The higher the "interest rate," the more you have to pay back beyond the amount you borrowed. This compounds over time, so if you borrowed $100 at an 8% interest rate, you'll have to pay back $108. If you don't pay back the full $108 that same month, you'll owe $116.60 the next month even though you didn't borrow any more money, and so on into infinity...)

Consider the avalanche method, where you pay off the highest interest debt first, or the snowball method, which targets smaller debts for quick wins. Making extra payments when possible can also help chip away at the principal (the base amount you originally borrowed, which continually accrues interest), reducing the amount of interest you'll pay over time. If your debts feel overwhelming, debt consolidation might be worth exploring. This involves combining multiple debts into one loan with a potentially lower interest rate, simplifying payments and possibly saving money in the long run. If you think you're in a position where you might need this help, talk to your bank for advice and do some research to learn about debt consolidation options.

Avoiding debt pitfalls is about foresight and awareness. Understanding the impact of interest rates is fundamental; they determine how much more you pay beyond the original loan. A lower rate can save you significant money over time. Unnecessary borrowing is another trap to avoid, as it can lead to a cycle of debt that's hard to escape. Before signing on the dotted line, read and understand loan terms to know exactly what you're agreeing to. If you are taking on a loan or any significant credit debt, make sure that you have a plan in place for how you will repay it as quickly as possible. Avoid relying on your credit card for emergencies. Building an emergency savings fund acts as a financial cushion, offering peace of mind and a buffer against unexpected expenses. It's your safety net, preventing you from having to rely on credit in a pinch.

Now, let's talk about the mysterious creature known as the credit score. This three-digit number wields significant power over your financial life. High credit scores can open doors to better loan terms  in the future and access to nicer rental properties or car loans with more budget-friendly repayment plans, while low credit scores might slam those opportunities shut. Several factors influence your score, with payment history being the heavyweight champion. Consistently paying bills on time shows lenders that you're reliable. Credit utilization, or how much of your available credit you're using, is another critical factor. Keeping this ratio low, ideally using under 30% of all the credit available to you, signals that you're not overly reliant on credit.

Regularly checking and monitoring your credit reports is vital. It's like having a regular health check-up for your finances. Look for errors or unfamiliar accounts that could negatively affect your score. If you find any discrepancies, report them immediately to the credit bureau. Steps to improve your credit score include paying bills promptly, reducing outstanding debt, and being strategic about new credit and loan applications. Each positive action adds a feather to your cap, enhancing your creditworthiness.

The long-term impact of credit scores extends beyond borrowing. They can influence insurance premiums, rental applications, and sometimes even job prospects. A good credit score can be your golden ticket to favorable financial opportunities, while a poor score might require you to jump through additional hoops. Understanding how your credit score works and actively managing it is an investment in your future. It's about building a solid foundation, so when opportunity knocks, you're ready to answer confidently (DeNicola, 2025).

Introduction to Investing for Beginners

So, you've got some cash sitting around, and you're wondering what to do with it. You could tuck it under your mattress, but let's be real, that's not doing much for you. Enter the world of investing. Think of investing as putting your money to work. Unlike saving, where your money sits quietly in a piggy bank, investing involves using that money to potentially earn more over time. It's like planting a money tree that could grow bigger and stronger with the right care. Why is investing important? Well, it's all about long-term financial growth. The magic of compound interest means your earnings can earn their own earnings, like a snowball rolling downhill, gathering more snow as it goes.

But before you get too excited, let's talk risks. Investing isn't a guaranteed win. Markets can be unpredictable, and there's always a chance you could lose money. That's why it's crucial to start early and give your investments time to recover from any bumps along the way. The earlier you start, the more time your investments have to grow and recover from downturns. It's like giving your money a head start in a marathon.

 Now, let's explore the different types of investments you might consider as a beginner. You've probably heard of stocks and bonds. Stocks are like buying a tiny piece of a company. If the company does well, you can profit. If it doesn't, you might lose some of your investment. Bonds, on the other hand, are like lending money to a company or government. They promise to pay you back with interest. Think of them as a more stable but potentially less lucrative option. For those who want a mix, mutual funds and ETFs (Exchange-Traded Funds) pool money from many investors to buy a diversified portfolio of stocks and bonds. They offer a way to invest in a variety of assets without picking individual stocks. They are also less likely to see extreme changes because the investment is being spread out in a lot of different places instead of putting all the eggs in one basket.

Real estate might sound like something for middle-aged men, but it's worth considering. Owning property can be a solid investment, creating the option to generate rental income and appreciating in value over time. And let's not forget retirement accounts like the Roth IRA. Even though you're years away from retiring, starting a Roth IRA early allows your contributions to grow tax-free. It's like planting seeds now for a mega future harvest at retirement. Your bank or financial institution can help you calculate your projected returns at retirement if you were to start investing now. Ask them about it!

Ready to start investing? First, you'll need to open a brokerage account. This is like setting up a bank account specifically for buying and selling investments. Many platforms cater to new investors with user-friendly interfaces and educational resources. Once your account is set up, it's time to research and select investments. Look for companies and funds that align with your interests and goals. Diversifying your portfolio is key. By spreading your investments across different assets, you reduce the risk of losing everything if one doesn't perform well.

Setting investment goals is another important step. Whether it's saving for college, a car, a dream vacation, or retirement some day, having clear goals helps guide your investment decisions. It's like having a roadmap for your financial journey. As you invest, you'll encounter terms like bull and bear markets. A bull market means prices are rising, while a bear market indicates they're falling. Dividends are payments some companies make to shareholders from their profits. Capital gains refer to the profit made from selling an investment. Market volatility describes how much prices fluctuate, and it's important to stay calm during these swings. Dollar-cost averaging is a strategy where you invest a fixed amount regularly, regardless of market conditions, which can help smooth out the impact of market fluctuations (Stalter & Schultz, 2024).

Investing might seem like a daunting world, but remember, you're not
alone. There are countless resources
and communities eager to help you
navigate the complexities. It's about
making informed decisions, taking
calculated risks, and learning as you go. As you start investing, you're
not just growing your wealth—you're building a foundation for financial independence. And who knows? With time, patience, and a
little luck, you might just find yourself with a thriving money tree.

*A note of clarification: the author is not a financial advisor nor a
tax professional. The content of this chapter is meant to be taken as
helpful advice from a friend, not legal or professional advice. The author
takes no responsibility for the success or failure of applying any of the
tax advice or financial strategies discussed here or in previous chapters.
Please contact a professional to get professional tax and financial advice.*

Chapter 15

Becoming a Legal Voter

W hen you come of age to legally vote in the US, it can be daunting to know where to start. Don't worry if you feel like you don't have all the answers. No one really does. But here's some basic tips to help you get started.

 First of all, you'll need to register to vote in your state in order to be sent a ballot when the next election comes around. You can do this online at https://vote.gov/register. Once you're registered, you will receive a ballot to your registered mailing address every time an election you are eligible to vote in happens; these will include federal, state, and local (county, city, or district) elections. Just because you receive a ballot doesn't mean you are required to vote, but you don't have the option to vote at all if you haven't registered yet so that you can receive ballots.

If you do vote, it's best if you plan ahead so that you can spend some time doing research about different candidates that are running or about the pros and cons of different laws that are being proposed for your county, city, or district. Often, you will receive a voter's guide in the mail when voting time comes, which gives more details about any law changes being proposed and lists out the pros and cons of the proposed changes. If not, you can usually find this information online. If you are looking for official information, use websites that end in ".gov."

Your ballot will have specific instructions inside about how and when it has to be turned in to be counted. Follow these instructions carefully. Also, always make sure to sign the outside of your ballot envelope with your full name, exactly as it is printed on the envelope, before turning in your ballot.

Otherwise, your vote won't be counted. And just like that, you're on your way to laying hold of your civic rights and contributing to the future of your city, state, and country!

Conclusion

Congratulations on making it through this journey of adulting! You've tackled everything from job hunting like a boss to whipping up a nutritious breakfast faster than a pop quiz. Adulting doesn't come with a video tutorial, but this book gives you a handy guide to navigate the chaos. You've learned how to create a realistic budget, save for both short and long-term goals, and make smart shopping choices. In the kitchen, you've gotten familiar with essential tools, mastered quick meals, and understood the importance of safety and hygiene. Time management now feels less like blundering through a game of rugby without knowing the rules and more like a well-rehearsed dance.

You've got the tools to balance school, work, and social life without losing your cool.

We've dived into the nitty-gritty of communication, tackling everything from active listening to conflict resolution. You now know how to express yourself constructively, resolve conflicts with grace, and maybe even enjoy public speaking a little more than before. Understanding emotions and building empathy have equipped

you to handle relationships with care and compassion, while internet safety tips help you navigate the digital world smartly.

Let's not forget the practical skills in household maintenance and automobile basics. Whether it's doing laundry like a pro or checking your car's oil levels, you're more prepared to handle life's everyday surprises. And with job tips under your belt, you're ready to step into the professional world with confidence.

All these skills are your toolkit for life. They're pretty much the equivalent of superpowers in the real world. Adulting is about making choices, learning from mistakes, and constantly evolving. The goal here is to turn these newfound skills into habits that will make your life easier, more fulfilling, and, dare I say, a tad more fun.

Now, it's time for action. Take what you've learned and put it into practice. Create that budget, plan those meals, and communicate effectively. Try changing that tire or cooking that new dish you've been eyeing. The only way to reinforce these skills is by doing. Don't be afraid to make mistakes—that's where the real learning happens. Every step you take is progress, and each small victory builds your confidence.

I hope you feel inspired to tackle whatever comes your way. Remember, you're not alone on this journey. We all have those days when adulting feels overwhelming, but you've got this! You have the tools, the knowledge, and the spirit to face anything life throws at you. Embrace the ups and downs and keep moving forward. You are more capable than you think, and your potential is limitless.

Thank you for allowing me to be a part of your journey. It's been a pleasure guiding you through the twists and turns of adulting. I'm grateful for your trust and eager to see how you use these skills to shape your future. Keep learning, keep growing, and remember to enjoy the ride. Here's to a life full  of success, growth, and a bit of humor along the way. You've got this!

Appendix of Recipes

Soft and Chewy Granola Bars

P rep Time: 20 min Cook time: 10 min Total Time: 30 min

Makes 12 bars

These homemade granola bars are much better than what you can buy at the store, especially since you can substitute your favorite dried fruit or nuts. You need to chill the bars for at least 2 hours before cutting them.

You Will Need:

2 ½ cups old fashioned rolled oats

1/2 cup whole almonds, coarsely chopped, or sliced almonds

1/3 cup pure honey

1/4 cup unsalted butter, cut into pieces

1/4 cup packed light brown sugar

1/2 teaspoon vanilla extract

1/4 teaspoon fine sea salt

1/2 cup dried cranberries (or other dried fruit of choice), coarsely chopped

1/4 cup plus 2 tablespoons mini chocolate chips

Directions:

1) Toast Oats and Nuts

Preheat the oven to 350°F. Line the bottom and sides of an 8-inch or 9-inch square pan with aluminum foil or parchment paper.

On a separate baking sheet, spread the oats and chopped almonds evenly and bake for 5 minutes. Stir and bake another 3 to 5 minutes or until lightly toasted. Transfer to a large bowl.

2) Make Bars

Combine the butter, honey, brown sugar, vanilla extract, and salt in a small saucepan over medium heat. Cook, stirring occasionally, until the butter melts, the mixture bubbles, and the sugar dissolves.

Pour the butter mixture into the bowl with toasted oats and almonds. Mix well. Let cool for 5 minutes.

Stir in the cranberries and 1/4 cup of the mini chocolate chips. Some of the chocolate chips might melt, but they turn into glue and help hold the bars together.

Transfer the oat mixture to the prepared baking pan with parchment or foil from earlier and press it into the pan firmly using a rubber spatula. Press hard so that the bars will stay together once cooled and cut. We press for about one minute to be extra safe.

Scatter the remaining 2 tablespoons of chocolate chips over the pressed granola mixture, and then use a rubber spatula to gently press them into the top.

Cover and refrigerate for at least 2 hours. Remove the block of granola mixture from the pan and peel away the foil or parchment. Cut into 12 bars.

3) Store Extras

Store granola bars in an airtight container. For softer bars, keep them in a cool area of your kitchen (like a dark pantry). For firmer bars, store in the fridge for up to three weeks. Bars will keep in the freezer for up to three months when wrapped well.

For the original recipe, visit Inspired Taste at the QR code.

Homemade Granola Bars

Prep Time: 5 mins Chilling Time: 2 hrs
Makes 8 Bars

These homemade granola bars are quick and delicious and naturally gluten-free!

Ingredients:

1 cup very smooth creamy natural peanut butter or cashew butter

⅔ cup honey

1 teaspoon vanilla extract

Heaping ½ teaspoon sea salt

2½ cups whole rolled oats

⅓ cup mini chocolate chips (or chopped up regular chocolate chips)

3 tablespoons pepitas, or crushed peanuts, or cashews

Instructions:

Line an 8x8 baking pan with parchment paper.

In a large bowl, stir together the peanut butter, honey, vanilla, and salt, until smooth.

Add the oats, chocolate chips and the pepitas (or nuts). The mixture might seem dry at first, but keep stirring and it'll come together. Stir to combine and press firmly into the pan. Use a second piece of parchment paper and the back of a measuring cup to help flatten the mixture. Chill for at least 2 hours, then slice into bars.

Store bars in the fridge in an airtight container.

For the original recipe, visit Love & Lemons at the QR code.

Easy Breakfast Egg Muffins

Prep Time: 15 mins Cook Time: 30 mins Total Time: 45 mins
Servings: 12 muffins

These breakfast egg muffins are inspired by your favorite morning casserole or omelet! They're great for an on-the-go breakfast and very customizable to your taste. You can substitute any vegetables, cheese, or meat that you like. I love to make a dozen of these and have them in my fridge to grab in the morning on my way to work.

Ingredients:

1 green bell pepper, chopped

1 red bell pepper, chopped

1 bunch green onions, chopped

8 large eggs

2 ¾ ounces fully-cooked bacon pieces

¼ cup whole milk (or milk substitute)

1 pinch garlic powder, or to taste

1 pinch onion powder, or to taste

salt and ground black pepper to taste

½ (8 ounce) package shredded mild Cheddar cheese

Directions:

Preheat the oven to 350 degrees F (175 degrees C). Grease a 12-cup muffin tin with cooking spray (if it's a nonstick surface) or butter (for all other materials).

Place bell peppers and green onions into a large bowl. Add eggs, bacon, milk, garlic powder, onion powder, salt, and pepper. Sprinkle Cheddar cheese into the bowl and whisk until incorporated. Pour mixture equally into the prepared muffin cups.

Bake in the preheated oven until a toothpick inserted into the center of a muffin comes out clean, about 30 minutes. Let cool slightly before serving. Store leftovers in an airtight container in the fridge for 1 week, or freeze in a freezer-safe bag for up to 1 month and reheat in the microwave.

For the original recipe, visit AllRecipes at the QR code.

3-Ingredient One Pot Pasta

Prep Time: 5 mins Cook Time: 40 mins Total Time: 45 mins

Servings 4

Just 3 ingredients is all you need to make this easy One Pot Pasta recipe! It's a cozy, comforting dish that you can make in just about 45 minutes with very little effort. A delicious meat sauce with your favorite pasta is cooked together in one pot for a flavorful, hearty, no-fuss meal!

Ingredients:

1 pound lean ground beef or turkey

1 teaspoon salt

1 jar (approx. 25 oz.) marinara sauce

12 ounces pasta (we like rotini, rigatoni, or farfalle)

Optional garnish: grated parmesan cheese and fresh basil leaves

Instructions:

Heat a large pot or Dutch oven over medium-high heat. Add beef. Cook, breaking beef into small pieces with a wooden spoon, until browned and cooked through, about 6 minutes. Add salt.

Reduce heat to medium and add marinara sauce to pot with beef. Fill empty marinara jar with water (approx. 3 cups) and add to the pot as well. Stir to combine. Add pasta and stir again.

Bring pasta and sauce to a simmer (just barely bubbling). Cook for 15 minutes, stirring frequently to ensure pasta does not stick to the bottom. Add 1 more cup water and continue cooking, stirring frequently, until pasta is tender, about 15 minutes more.

Garnish with parmesan and fresh basil. Serve immediately.

Notes: You can also optionally slice and sauté veggies like bell pepper, onion, zucchini, or mushrooms ahead of time and add those in for the last 10 minutes that your pasta and sauce are cooking.

Once prepared, this pasta dish will keep in the fridge for about 5 days. To reheat the pasta, add it to the stove with a splash of olive oil, water, or broth and heat until warm. You can also rewarm individual servings in the microwave.

For the original recipe, visit Kim's Cravings at the QR code.

Quick Beef Stir-Fry

Prep Time: 15 mins Cook Time: 10 mins Total Time: 25 mins

Servings: 4

Quick and easy beef stir-fry recipe. I make this on my busiest weeknights.

Ingredients:

2 tablespoons vegetable oil

1 pound beef sirloin, cut into 2-inch strips (or chicken breast, sliced in strips)

1 ½ cups fresh broccoli florets

1 red bell pepper, cut into matchsticks

2 carrots, thinly sliced

1 green onion, chopped

1 teaspoon minced garlic

2 tablespoons soy sauce

2 tablespoons sesame seeds, toasted

Directions:

Gather all ingredients.

Heat vegetable oil in a large wok or skillet over medium-high heat; add beef and stir-fry until browned, 3 to 4 minutes (10-12 minutes if using chicken).

Move beef to the side of the wok and add broccoli, bell pepper, carrots, green onion, and garlic to the center of the wok; stir-fry vegetables for 2 minutes.

Stir beef into vegetables and season with soy sauce and sesame seeds. Continue to cook and stir until vegetables are tender, about 2 more minutes.

Serve hot and enjoy! This goes great served over rice. (Just follow the directions on your bag of rice to cook. Start the rice first if it isn't instant rice, as it will take longer to cook.)

For the original recipe, visit AllRecipes at the QR code.

Sheet Pan Sausage And Veggies

Prep Time: 10 mins Cook Time: 35 mins Total Time: 45 mins
Servings: 4

This one-pan, incredibly simple to make, Sheet Pan Sausage And Veggies makes this the absolute perfect meal for any weekday dinner. With virtually no mess, this quick and nutritious recipe is a family favorite.

Ingredients:

2 cups baby potatoes washed and patted dry

1 medium broccoli head cut into florets

2 medium bell peppers any color, cut into 1 inch pieces

2 cups cherry tomatoes

1 pound smoked sausage, chicken, turkey, pork, or beef sliced into ¼-inch slices

¼ cup olive oil

1 tablespoon Italian seasoning

1 teaspoon garlic powder

½ teaspoon salt or to taste

½ teaspoon pepper or to taste

¼ cup Parmesan cheese grated, optional

Instructions:

1) Preheat the oven: Preheat the oven to 400°F. Line a large baking sheet with parchment paper.

2) Combine ingredients: Place all the veggies (tomatoes excluded) and sausage on the prepared sheet pan. Drizzle the olive oil all over everything, then add the Italian seasoning, garlic powder, salt, pepper

and toss everything together well. Arrange them so that they are one even layer over the baking sheet, to ensure even cooking.

3) Bake: Transfer the baking sheet to the oven and bake for 15 minutes.

4) Add tomatoes: Carefully remove the baking sheet from the oven and add the tomatoes. Flip or stir all the ingredients around. Return the baking sheet to the oven and bake for another 20 minutes or until the vegetables are crisp-tender and potatoes are fork tender.

5) Finish and serve: If desired, sprinkle with freshly grated Parmesan cheese as soon as they come out of the oven and serve over rice or quinoa.

Notes: By lining the baking sheet with parchment paper, you'll get the quickest cleanup possible. Simply discard the parchment paper when done, give the baking sheet a quick rinse and cleanup is all done.

Other veggies that are also great in this dish include zucchini, asparagus, green beans, brussels sprouts, onion, sweet potatoes, or carrots.

Make sure the vegetables and meat are not crowded on the pan; otherwise, they may take longer to cook. They can also steam instead of roast if they are crowded, which is not the outcome we are looking for. Use 2 pans if needed.

Feel free to add some of your favorite herbs and spices. If you like some heat, add in red pepper flakes to kick it up a notch, or include some dried oregano, basil, thyme or parsley.

Cut all the vegetables roughly the same size, as this will ensure they cook at the same rate.

Store cooled veggies and sausage in an airtight container and place in the refrigerator for up to 3 days. For the original recipe, visit Jo Cooks at the QR code.

References

10 tips for planning meals on a budget - Unlock food. (n.d.). https://www.unlockfood.ca/en/Articles/Budget/10-Tips-for-Planning-Meals-on-a-Budget.aspx.

AAA. (2023). *How to jump-start a car*. Retrieved from https://www.aaa.com/autorepair/articles/how-to-jump-start-a-car.

Aacap. (n.d.). *Stress management and teens*. https://www.aacap.org/AACAP/Families_and_Youth/Facts_for_Families/FFF-Guide/Helping-Teenagers-With-Stress-066.

A Teens Guide to social media safety. (2024, October 26). Safe Search Kids. https://www.safesearchkids.com/a-teens-guide-to-social-media-safety/.

Advice for teens: Manage your digital footprint | UME Digital Literacy. (2023, July 12). UME Digital Literacy. https://marylandersonline.umd.edu/resources/advice-teens-manage-your-digital-footprint.

Bank of America. (2024, October 3). *How to read a paycheck or pay stub*. Better Money Habits. https://bettermoneyhabits.bankofamerica.com/en/taxes-income/how-to-read-a-paycheck.

Blake, K., Brown, T., & Finch, S. (2024, April 22). *First Time Apartment Renter's Guide: 20 step Checklist*. https://www.apartmentlist.com/renter-life/first-time-renter-apartment-guide-checklist.

Blue light has a dark side. (2024, July 4). Harvard Health Publishing. https://www.health.harvard.edu/staying-healthy/blue-light-has-a-dark-side.

Breathing techniques for stress relief. (n.d.). WebMD. https://www.webmd.com/balance/stress-management/stress-relief-breathing-techniques.

Buttonow, J. (2020, August 19). *Tax deductions and credits for young adults | H&R Block*. H&R Block. https://www.hrblock.com/tax-center/filing/adjustments-and-deductions/tax-deductions-for-young-adults/.

Caldera, L. (2024, November 12). *Best budgeting apps for teens (I tried them all) - Kids' money*. Kids' Money. https://www.kidsmoney.org/teens/budgeting/apps/.

Chan, K. (2023, May 19). *Sympathy vs. Empathy: What's the Difference?* Verywell Mind. https://www.verywellmind.com/sympathy-vs-empathy-whats-the-difference-7496474.

Consumer Reports. (2023). *How to clean your dryer vent*. https://www.consumerreports.org/home-maintenance/cleaning-your-dryer-vent.

Cook's Illustrated. (2023). *How to sharpen a kitchen knife*. https://www.cooksillustrated.com/articles.

Credit cards for young adults | FDIC.gov. (n.d.). https://www.fdic.gov/consumer-resource-center/2023-08/credit-cards-young-adults.

Des Moines Symphony. (2024, February 8). *How Classical Music Improves Mental Health*. https://www.dmsymphony.org/about/news/how-classical-music-improves-mental-health.

DeNicola, L. (2025, February 18). *Credit Score Basics: Everything you need to know*. https://www.experian.com/blogs/ask-experian/credit-education/score-basics/understanding-credit-scores/.

Digital, T. (2023, August 25). *15 Home repair and maintenance skills Every homeowner should know*. Window World of St. Louis. https://www.windowworldstlouis.com/blog/basic-home-repair-skills/.

Doyle, A. (2024, June 19). *Teen job interview questions, answers, and tips*. The Balance. https://www.thebalancemoney.com/teen-job-interview-questions-and-best-answers-2063882.

Equal Employment Opportunity Commission. (2023). *Filing a charge of discrimination*. https://www.eeoc.gov/filing-charge-discrimination.

Equal Employment Opportunity Commission. (2023). *Sexual Harassment*. *https://www.eeoc.gov/sexual-harassment*.

Exercise Intensity: How to measure it. (2023, August 5). Mayo Clinic. https://www.mayoclinic.org/healthy-lifestyle/fitness/in-dep th/exercise-intensity/art-20046887.

Fear of public speaking: How can I overcome it? (n.d.). Mayo Clinic. https://www.mayoclinic.org/diseases-conditions/specific-phobia s/expert-answers/fear-of-public-speaking/faq-20058416.

Goldberg, E. (2016, October 31). 10 essential kitchen tools for beginner cooks. *Bon Appétit*. https://www.bonappetit.com/story/1 0-essential-kitchen-tools-beginner-cooks.

Haydon, S. (2024, July 1). *The 7 best time management apps for students*. Study Work Grow. https://studyworkgrow.com/the-7-bes t-time-management-apps-for-students/.

How important is an oil change? (2024, May 7). Progressive. https ://www.progressive.com/lifelanes/importance-of-oil-changes/.

How to handle peer pressure. (n.d.). Fairfax County Public Schools. https://www.fcps.edu/student-wellness-tips/peer-pressure.

Internet safety: Creating strong passwords. (n.d.). GCFGlobal. org. https://edu.gcfglobal.org/en/internetsafety/creating-strong-pas swords/1/.

Jivanjee, P., Jr., Brennan, E., Gonzalez-Prats, M. C., & Transition Training Collaborative. (2016). *Building community supports for young people in the Transition years: A tip sheet for service providers.* https://www.pathwaysrtc.pdx.edu/pdf/projPTTP-Community-Support-Tip-Sheet.pdf.

Karr, W. B. A. (2024, July 31). *Why it's important to save money at an early age | MyDoh.* Mydoh. https://www.mydoh.ca/learn/money-101/money-basics/why-kids-and-teens-should-start-saving-money-early/.

Keep food safe! Food Safety Basics | Food Safety and Inspection Service. (n.d.). https://www.fsis.usda.gov/food-safety/safe-food-handling-and-preparation/food-safety-basics/steps-keep-food-safe.

Leverette, M. M. (2024, August 3). *How to do laundry in 10 easy steps.* The Spruce. https://www.thespruce.com/how-to-do-laundry-2146149.

Lodge Cast Iron. (2023). *Caring for your cast iron.* https://www.lodgecastiron.com/cleaning-and-care.

Martin, A. (2025, February 28). *What to know about buying a car for your teenager.* Bankrate. https://www.bankrate.com/loans/auto-loans/buying-a-car-for-your-teenager/.

Melrose, J. (2024, September 10). *50 breakfast ideas for teens: easy, quick, and healthy options!* The Melrose Family. https://thenymelrosefamily.com/breakfast-ideas-for-teens/.

Morris, G. (2024, July 11). *How to save money on utilities*. InCharge Debt Solutions. https://www.incharge.org/financial-literacy/budge ting-saving/how-to-save-money-on-electric-gas-water-bill/.

Murray, K. (2023). *How to clean and season cast iron like a pro.* https://www.foodnetwork.com/how-to-clean-cast-iron.

National Center for Education Statistics (NCES). (2017). *Percentage of 2011–12 First Time Postsecondary Students Who Had Ever Declared a Major in an Associate's or Bachelor's Degree Program Within 3 Years of Enrollment, by Type of Degree Program and Control of First Institution: 2014*. Institute of Education Sciences, U.S. Department of Education. Washington, DC. https://nces.ed.gov/Datalab/Table sLibrary/TableDetails/11764.

National Credit Union Administration. (2023). *What is a credit union?* https://www.ncua.gov/consumers/what-credit-union.

Pacheco, D., & Pacheco, D. (2024, March 8). *Bedroom environment: What elements are important?* Sleep Foundation. https://www.sleepfoundation.org/bedroom-environment.

Patchin, J. W. & Hinduja, S. (2024). *2023 Cyberbullying Data.* Cyberbullying Research Center. https://cyberbullying.org/2023-cy berbullying-data.

Peterson, A. (2023). *The best ways to sharpen kitchen knives.* https ://www.foodandwine.com/how-to-sharpen-kitchen-knives.

Physical Activity Guidelines for School-Aged Children and Adolescents. (2024, July 3). Physical Education and Physical Activity. https://www.cdc.gov/physical-activity-education/guidelines/?CDC _AAref_Val=https://www.cdc.gov/healthyschools/physicalactivity/g uidelines.htm.

Pollack, J. (2024, September 18). *5 Essential conflict resolution skills for students (Kids & teens) | AllWin Conflict Resolution Training.* AllWin Conflict Resolution Training. https://conflict-resolution-tr aining.com/blog/conflict-resolution-skills-for-students/.

Raeburn, A. (2024, October 14). Pomodoro Technique 101: Get more done in Less time [2024] • Asana. *Asana.* https://asana.com/r esources/pomodoro-technique.

Rape, Abuse & Incest National Network. (2023). *National sexual assault hotline.* https://www.rainn.org/about-national-sexual-assaul t-hotline.

Ray, A. (2022, April 17). *SMART Goals and your teen - the Blue Heart Foundation.* The Blue Heart Foundation. https://thebluehea rtfoundation.org/smart-goals-and-your-teen/.

Reyell, B. (2024, December 6). *Workplace Etiquette: 21 Dos and Don'ts of the Workplace.* Northeastern University Graduate Programs. https://graduate.northeastern.edu/resources/workplace-etiquette/.

Safe Minimum Internal Temperature Chart | Food Safety and Inspection Service. (2020, May

11). https://www.fsis.usda.gov/food-safety/safe-food-handling-and
-preparation/food-safety-basics/safe-temperature-chart.

Sharma, S., Khandelwal, R., Yadav, K., Ramaswamy, G., & Vohra,
K. (2021). Effect of cooking food in iron pot and with iron ingot on
increase in hemoglobin level and iron content of the food. *Deleted
Journal*, *11*(2), 994–1005. https://doi.org/10.3126/nje.v11i2.36682.

Stalter, K., & Schultz, J. (2024, June 13). Investing for teens:
How to invest money as a teenager. *US News & World Report*. https://money.usnews.com/investing/articles/investing-for-tee
ns-how-to-invest-money-as-a-teenager.

Team Asana. (2025, January 29). The Eisenhower Matrix: How to
Prioritize Your To-Do List [2025] • Asana. *Asana*. https://asana.co
m/resources/eisenhower-matrix.

Teentalk. (2017). *Active listening worksheets*. https://teentalk.ca/
wp-content/uploads/2014/05/Active-Listening-Worksheets-16.pdf.

Top ten job search tips for teens | CareerForce. (2024, April
8). https://www.careerforcemn.com/careerforce-blog/top-ten-job-s
earch-tips-teens.

Travelers. (2023, February 20). *8 important car
maintenance services teens and new drivers need to
know*. https://www.travelers.com/resources/auto/maintenance/8-i
mportant-car-maintenance-services-teens-need-to-know.

Understanding and overcoming procrastination. (n. d.). McGraw Center for Teaching and Learning. https://mcgraw.princeton.edu/undergraduates/resources/resource-library/understanding-and-overcoming-procrastination.

U.S. Fire Administration. (2023). *Clothes dryer fire safety*. https://www.usfa.fema.gov/prevention/outreach/clothes_dryer_fires.html.

What does screen time do to my brain? | SUNY Potsdam. (2025). SUNY Potsdam. https://www.potsdam.edu/studentlife/wellness/counseling-center/what-does-screen-time-do-my-brain.

Whetzel, C. (2024, August 15). *Over half of iron deficiency cases in large health system still unresolved at three years*. Hematology.org. https://www.hematology.org/newsroom/press-releases/2024/over-half-of-iron-deficiency-cases-in-large-health-system-still-unresolved-at-three-years.